HISTORICISING HISTORY

AN EXPEDITION TO THE PAST

HISTORICISING HISTORY

AN EXPEDITION TO THE PAST

Editors

Dr. T. Anitha
Dr. Meera M. R.
Dr. R. Janatha Kumari

AUTHORSPRESS

Worldwide Circulation through Authorspress Global Network
First Published in 2023
by
Authorspress
Q-2A Hauz Khas Enclave, New Delhi-110 016 (India)
Phone: (0) 9818049852
E-mail: authorspressgroup@gmail.com
Website: www.authorspressbooks.com

Historicising History: An Expedition to the Past
ISBN 978-93-5529-531-6

Printed in India at Thomson Press (India) Limited

Preface

History is something that always connect us with our culture. It is something that help us to remember our past. People tend to do better once they become educated about their past. Learning about our past helps us learn about humanities own reflection and what is good or bad about it. It is important to study history because it teaches us about not only our own culture but the culture of the whole world. History is the way of understanding human life and helping us embrace new ways of making a new and healthier lifestyle. Knowing our past is something that becomes an asset to build our future in a better way. Studying history help us understand how events in the past made things the way they are today. With lessons from the past, we not only learn about ourselves and how we came to be, but also develop the ability to avoid mistakes and create better paths for societies. History provides us with the data that is used to create laws, of theories about various aspects of society. This book unveils the mysteries, embraces the miracles and envelops the reality of the past. It strengthens the sense of identity of the nation.

The various research articles that deal with the glory and achievements of our nation becomes the hall mark of the book. Movements for better perspectives are intertwined with those of religion, tourism, and society. The current volume examines the interaction between society and religion and how it has an impact. Moreover, it views tourism as a current component power. The Khaddar movement, which is intertwined with national spirit and self-respect, is described in detail. Rajaji's Khadar movement helped to partially ease the country's hunger problem by encouraging the work ethic of the underprivileged. Similar efforts are made to shed light on the life of Mr. K. Perumal Panikar, a little-known liberation warrior from Kottar. An article about movement Women began to make their mark at the end of the nineteenth century, first locally and later nationally. It shows how the women's movement's support base grew as a result of women's involvement in the struggle for freedom.

The predicament of Dalit women in India is described in an equivalent narrative. The accomplishments of Savitribai Phule, who sought to end violence against women, is also highlighted. The greatest obstacle to human development is the violation of human rights. A thorough account of the issues faced by women in the community of people with disabilities is provided.

As deeply ingrained in society as religious belief are superstitions, taboos, and traditions. It sheds information on the psychological feelings of inferiority inflicted upon the depressed classes and how Portuguese Jesuits used this to their advantage by converting the low caste individuals to Christianity. Similar to that, a study is being written that will analyse the Church's mission from a comprehensive angle and show how people's daily lives reflect religious principles. Religion has an impact on social confidence and cognition. An example from the Hindu temple of Cheranmahadevi is given to support this claim. In a paper, a thorough report about India's Sleepless City is also presented. Madurai is a popular destination for pilgrims from all over the world. The city of Madurai is the best illustration of religious cooperation because it is populated by Jains, Muslims, and Christians. Respect is shown for each other's respective religious convictions.

There is a detailed account of beaches of Kanya Kumari's district. The beautiful beaches of Kanya Kumari have lush greenery, dense coconut plantations along the shore, and shallow sea waves. Similar narration is provided for Kumarakom as a visitor and environment-friendly destination. A full description of how responsible tourism is envisioned in Kumarakom is also debated in a paper. To bridge the gap between Goa's colonial past and the autonomous present, a paper on colonial influence in Katharina Kakar's Goa is presented. It also looks at how the roughly 450-year colonial occupation of Goa affected its culture, food, and architectural style. A paper explores remarkable descriptions of paintings and serves as a reminder of cultural influences. Together with other early painted pottery creations, it is addressed how the tradition of painted pottery travelled from Afghanistan and Baluchistan to India.

We are deeply indebted to the contributors who have rendered helping hands to this academic venture through their valuable contribution. We humbly remember with gratitude our Principal Dr. K. V. Jayashree, our Management and all the kind souls who have been with us throughout this project. We thank Sudarshan Kcherry, CEO, Authorspress, New Delhi for the support to make our endeavour successful.

Dr. T. Anitha

Contents

1

A Study on Impact of Empowerment Programmes for Differently Abled Women in Thiruvananthapuram District

Dr Pradeesh S

Introduction

In modern society acting independently is of supreme importance, whether it is in the area of day to day activities, personal care, cooking, studies, or for that matter anything requires human endeavour or pursuit. In all these areas differently abled persons faces lot of discrimination socially, economically, psychologically and emotionally. His incapacity generates emotional problems and tends to isolate himself from society (Sunder.S, 2010). Empowerment reduces the impact of various problems and discriminations faced by the differently abled people. Typically empowerment occurs for a specific period of time, but can involve single or multiple interventions delivered by an individual or team of empowerment workers and can be needed from the acute or initial phase immediately following recognition of a health condition through post-acute and maintenance phases. Empowerment is a set of measures that help differently abled people to achieve and maintain optimal functioning in interaction with their environment. (World Report on Disability, 2011). In other words empowerment is the restoration of the handicapped person physically, mentally, socially and vocationally to the fullest extends compatible with his abilities and disabilities. Various goals of empowerment are orientation, physical independence, mobility, occupational integration, social integration, economic self-sufficiency (Sunder.S, 2010). No person is said to be fully rehabilitated unless and until all the above criteria have been satisfied. Thus, empowerment refers to the services and technologies that are made available to people with disabilities so that they might learn to adapt to their world (Deegan, Patricia.E, 1988) According to various estimates, about 5 to 10 per cent of the world population is affected by one or more disabilities. Census of India 2011 reports that 26 million people in India are differently abled persons. It forms 2.22% of the total population of the country. Out of them 11.8 million are females. As per 2011 Census, in Kerala 7.61 lakh of people are differently abled which forms 2.28% of the total population. Out of them 3.67 lakh are females (Census of India, 2011).

Among the differently abled community, Women with disabilities are multiply disadvantaged through their status as women and as persons with disabilities and majority of them are unemployed and living in poverty. They are always exposed to lot of stereotyping within their communities, which make them feel devalued, isolated and ashamed and this in turn results denial of their basic human rights. Lack of access to health care will aggravate their disability and it makes quick empowerment difficult and ensures that their position will not improve. There is very little public consciousness of the need to integrate them to the main stream of development. Government of India along with various departments provides lot of various policy interventions and empowerment programmes for the welfare and integration of the differently abled people, but at the grass root level effectiveness of these programmes is less. So a more realistic and pragmatic approach is needed to empower them not just economically but in a more basic and meaningful sense.

Objectives of the study

1. To examine at primary level whether the differently abled women have awareness about various programmes and policies for them.
2. To analyse various services availed by differently abled women and whether these benefits are satisfactory at primary level.
3. To review various legislations, policies and empowerment programmes for the differently abled people by the governmental bodies

4. To examine the income, educational and occupational status of differently abled women at primary level.

Methodology of the Study

The evaluation of empowerment programmes for differently abled women, both primary and secondary data are used. Secondary data is collected from various census reports, NSSO rounds, health reports, official websites etc. Primary data is collected from Thiruvanthapuram District in a rural-urban comparative basis. Thiruvanthapuram district is selected for collecting the primary data because as per various census reports, Thiruvananthapuram District has the highest number of differently abled population and also the highest number of female differently abled population. Data is collected through random sampling technique from the families of 120 differently abled women in the district. 60 samples from Thiruvananthapuram Corporation and 30 samples each from Parrasala Panchayt and Kadinamkulam Panchayat. Hence the study is based on 120 households having 120 differently abled women and 102 non-differently abled women. Out of 102 non-differently abled women, 54 represent urban area and 48 represent rural areas. Appropriate statistical techniques are also used to analyse the data.

Legislations, Policy Interventions and Empowerment Programmes for Differently abled people

In India welfare and empowerment of persons with disabilities has gained importance since independence. The following efforts have been combined, expanded and oriented towards empowerment and integration of persons with disabilities.

Legislations for the differently abled people

In the post-independence period the govt. of India recognised the fact that the differently abled have also equal right to participate in social and economic activities along with others in the society. This recognition of basic rights of the differently abled led to guaranteed provision under Article 41 in the Indian constitution adopted for the first time in 1950. The government of India has included the "Welfare of the Handicapped" in the Nation's five year plans by realising that the handicapped constitute a part of the weaker sections of the society. The Article 41 and 46 of the Indian Constitution insist on the welfare of the differently abled persons.

Specific Acts

The Indian Lunacy Act, 1912 deals with the mentally differently abled in India. Under the provisions of the Act, the policies are empowered to arrest wandering lunatics. The Lepers Act, 1899, deals with the problems of lepers. Section VI of the Act empowers the State Governments to arrest pauper lepers without warrant (Barik, S, 2009).

The Mental Health Act 1987

The Mental Health Act replaced the Indian Lunacy Act 1912 and came into effect in all states and UT's of India in 1993. This act consolidated and amended the law relating to the treatment and care of mentally ill persons and to make better provisions. (WHO, 2006)

Provisions in General laws

Apart from these specific Acts pertaining to two categories of the differently abled there are regulations relating to differently abled in a number of laws concerning the general population. (Barik, S, 2009).The following are a few examples:

- *Representation of peoples Act, 1950:* Section 60 provides that a citizen ought to be mentally sound in order to be an eligible voter.
- *Indian Contract Act:* Under section 12, a contract entered into by an unsound mind is void even if a person has attained the age of majority.
- *Hindu Marriage Act:* It prohibits marriages where one of the parties is a lunatic at the time of marriage.
- *Hindu Section Act, 1956:* It stipulates that unsoundness of mind is not a bar to inheritance of property.
- *Indian Penal Code*: Section 84 stipulates that nothing is an offence which is done by a person who at the time of doing it, by reason of unsoundness of mind, is incapable of knowing the nature of the Act or that he is doing what it is either wrong or contrary to law.
- *Labour Laws:* An analysis of the provisions of the labour laws in the country shows that laws such as the payment of wages Act, 1965, payment of Bonus Act, 1965, Industrial Disputes Act, 1947, the factories Act, 1948 and Minimum Wages Act,

1948, do not apparently discriminate between normal persons and differently abled persons.

- *The Educational Law:* The right to education is available to all citizens including the differently abled. Article 29 of the constitution guarantees the admission of every citizen including differently abled in to any educational institution maintained by state. Further the Constitution directs the state to provide free and compulsory education for all children including the differently abled up to the age of 14 years.
- *Family Law (Matrimonial):* The laws relating to marriage are uniform to differently abled and non-differently abled class. There is no bar in respect of differently abled persons having relation with the non-differently abled persons provided both are of marriageable age and do not suffer from mental illness.
- *The Succession Law:* The differently abled are not deprived of succession or inheritance to property. The physical inability or deformity would not disentitle a person for inheriting ancestral property.
- *Income Tax Laws*: The Income tax Act of 1961recognises the plight of the differently abled and allows concessions to the blinds or to those subjected to permanent physical disability or subjected to mental retardation and also allows deductions incurred on the maintenance of the differently abled
- *The Disabilities Act, 1995:* The person with disabilities (Equal opportunities, Protection of Rights and full participation) and equality of the people with disabilities in the Asian and pacific region passed in Beijing conference to which India was a signatory. The 1995 Act defines the responsibilities of the Central and State Governments with regard to the publically provided services for the differently abled persons. The Act provides lot of provisions to people with disabilities so that they can integrate to the main stream of development, individually and collectively (PWD Act, 1995).
- *Empowerment Council of India Act, 1992:* It deals with the development of manpower providing empowerment services. RCI was set up by the GOI in 1992, to regulate and standardise training policies and programmes in the field of empowerment for the Persons with

- *Disabilities.* The aim is to protect and promote economic and social rights of the people with disabilities.(RCI Act, 1992)
- *National Trust for Welfare of Persons with autism, cerebral palsy, mental retardation and Multiple Disability Act, 1999* has provisions for legal guardianship of the four categories and creation of enabling environment for as much independent living as possible (National Trust Act, 1999)

Policies and Preventive Interventions

Many of the more commonly seen disabilities are curable and can be addressed through an appropriate preventive, curative and a rehabilitative health care system. The coverage and reach of health care system is however a serious constraint on addressing the problem of disability in our country especially in the rural areas. More importantly, a critical element of public and social intervention namely, physical and social empowerment programmes for differently abled suffers on account of lack of adequate resources and integration with medical and other treatment and also from social insensitivity.

Building Synergies in Public Action for Addressing Disability

Government of India has undertaken after independence multiple programmes of education, training and empowerment for both the physically and mentally handicapped. 'The Ministry of Social Justice and Empowerment is the apex body that initiate and co-ordinate programmes for the welfare of the handicapped in the country. The 'Disability Division' of the Ministry of Social Justice & Empowerment is converted it into a separate Department named Department of Disability Affairs (Nishaktata Karya Vibhag) so that it can act as a link between all the other concerned Ministries/ Departments and fulfil its responsibilities towards the differently abled community. There are more than half a dozen Government Departments, which are directly engaged in addressing the problem of disability in India. Some of the public programmes on addressing disability issues are described here.

Health and Family Welfare

1. Child immunisation programmes
2. Leprosy eradication programmes

3. Blindness control programme and curative treatment of cataracts.

Department of Education

a) Integrated education for differently abled in special schools
b) Teachers Training programmes for persons with disabilities
c) Provision of books, uniforms, and other materials to school going differently abled

Ministry of Labour

i. Vocational empowerment centres for the differently abled.
ii. Training for promotion of employed of disables

Ministry of Urban Development

- Model norms and space standards for barrier free in built environment.

Ministry of Rural Development

- Reservation of 2-3 per cent benefits in all poverty alleviation schemes for the differently abled and for improving their environment by building barrier free infrastructure.

Ministry of Social Justice and Empowerment

- Monitoring implementation of persons with disability Act 1995.
- National programme for empowerment of persons with disabilities in States.
- Setting up composite resource centres, empowerment centres and National thrust for persons with various disabilities viz. Spinal injuries, Autism, cerebral palsy etc.

Department of Personnel and Training

- Implementation of 3% reservation of Government jobs for differently abled.

Department of Women and Child Development

- Training of Anganwadi workers and ANM for early defection and timely prevention of disabilities.

(Source: – National Human Development Report, 2001)

Government of India has established "National Institutes" for various types of disability with the objective of providing national level facilities in research, training, documentation and consultancy. These national institutes are (Walia, Gagandeep Kaur, 2014)

i. National Institute for the visually Handicapped (NIVH), Dehradun

ii. National Institute for the orthopedically Handicapped (NIOH), Kolkata

iii. National Institute for the Hearing Handicapped (NIHH), Mumbai

iv. National Institute for the Mentally Handicapped (NIMH), Secundrabad

v. National Institute of Speech and Hearing (NISH), Thiruvananthapuram

The following concessions and welfare schemes are available for the benefits of differently abled. The programmes are

- *Concessions in the railways*: Railways allow differently abled persons to travel at concession fares up to 75%in the first and second classes. Escorts accompanying blind, orthopedically and mentally handicapped persons are also eligible to75% concessions in the basic fare
- *Air Travel Concessions:* Indian airlines allow 50% concession fares to blind persons on single journeys.
- *Postage:* Payment of postage both inland and foreign for transmission by post of "Blind Literature" packets is exempted if send surface route.
- *Telecommunication:* Telephone facilities to blind persons on concessional and priority basis are provided on the following terms.

i. Rental Rebate: 50% of the normal rental.

ii. Advance Rental: 50% of the annual advance rental and bi-monthly rental as applicable to a private subscriber. This facility is available only in the non-oyt (special) category only preference in the allotment of public STD/PCO facilities to the handicapped persons.

- *Customs/Excise:* Braille paper are exempted from excise and customs duty provided the paper is supplied direct to a school for the blind or to a Braille press against an indent placed by the National Institute for Visually Handicapped, Dehradun.
- *Conveyance Allowance:* All central government employees who are blind or orthopedically handicapped are granted conveyance at 5% of basic pay.
- *Educational Allowance:* Reimbursement of tuition fee of physically and mentally handipped children of the central government employees.
- *Income Tax Concessions:* The Income Tax Act, 1961 provides deductionto the extent of Rs. 50,000/- for person who suffers fromnot less than 40 per cent of any disabilityand in case of severe disability to the extent of Rs. 100,000.Budget 2015 proposed50, 000/- to Rs. 75,000 and for person with severe disability from Rs.100,000 to Rs.125000.
- *Award of dealership by oil companies:* The ministry of petroleum and natural gas has reserved 7.5% of all types of dealership of the public sector companies for the orthopedically handicapped and blind persons. Similarly, the ministry has also reserved 7.5% of such dealership for defence personnel and those severely differently abled either in war or while on duty in pace time.
- *Employment of the handicapped*: Assistance of the differently abled persons in getting gainful employment is available either through the special cells in normal employment exchanges or through special employment exchanges for physically handicapped.
- *Reservation of jobs and other facilities for differently abled persons:* As per the orders of GOI, reservation of 3 %(basing on the category of handicapped) jobs have been made in Grade C and Grade D Posts for the physically handicapped persons. Some of the vacancies are earmarked for differently abled basing on the category 34th, 67thand 100th in a 100 vacancy cycle for blind, deaf, orthopedically handicapped respectively. The state governments are following the norms in the recruitments.

- *Scheme of assistance to differently abledpersons:* To assist the needy, physically handicapped persons with durable, modern and standard aids and appliances.
- *Scheme for national scholarship of persons with disabilities:* This scheme provides 500 scholarships every year for post-matric professional and technical courses through institutions. Students suffering from cerebral palsy, mental retardation, hearing impairments and multiple handicapped can get scholarship from 9th standard onwards.
- *National award for the welfare of persons with disabilities:* In 1969, the Government of India approved a scheme for giving national awards to the outstanding employers of persons with disabilities. Fifty one awardson various categories such as outstanding individuals and institutions will also be given.
- *Deendayal differently abled empowerment schemes:* The scheme provide support to NGO's to deliver various empowerment services to persons with disabilities. The activities undertaken are special schools, vocational training centres, community based empowerment programmes, half way homes for psycho-social empowerment, pre-school and early intervention programmes, manpower development etc.

Economic Assistance

- *Public Sector Banks:* Under the "Scheme of Public Sector Banks for Orphanages, Women's home and Physically Handicapped persons", the benefits extending by the banks with differential rate of interest to physically handicapped persons.
- *Subsidy to Differently abled Under Swarnajayanthi Grama Swarozgar Yojana (SGSY):* 3% quota is earmarked for the differently abled persons under the SGSY. This scheme is being implemented by the District Rural Development Agencies (DDRC's) along with Panchayat Raj Institutions, the Banks, and non-government organisation.
- *Financial Assistance Available to Persons with Disabilities:* The National Handicapped Finance and Development Corporation (NHFDC) have been incorporated by the Ministry of Social Justice and Empowerment, Government of India. It runs several schemes to financially assist the

differently abled persons who are eligible for this purpose. For sanctioning the financial assistance some eligibility conditions were prescribed, who fulfils all the conditions, they are sanctioning amounts.

- *Indira Awas Yojana (IAY):* 3% of IAY funds are reserved for the benefits of differently abled persons living below the poverty line in rural areas. The financial allocation should be utilised properly. Monitoring on these schemes should be required to know effective utilisation.

Apart from the above government schemes, the Rajiv Gandhi Foundation was also undertaken some welfare programmes for the differently abled persons. It also started a differently abled person's welfare unit in may1992.Since its inception; it has actively promoted the cause of the differently abled through various projects and programmes across the country. Even though there are lot of empowerment programmes, it is disheartening that Government have yet to reach large number of differently abled people in remote areas with sustainable empowerment services. These populations are yet to benefit from the vast potential of IT revolution to the full extend.

Results and Discussion

Classification of family on the basis of Income

Table 1 shows the classification on the basis of various income groups:

Table 1 Classification of family on the basis of income

Various Income	No. of Rural respondents		No. of Urban respondents		Total	
	Differently abled	Non-differently abled	Differently abled	Non-differently abled	Differently abled	Non-differently abled
Low income group (Below 10,000)	27 (45)	21 (43.75)	14 (23.33)	11 (20.37)	41 (34.16)	32 (31.37)
Middle Income group (10,000-20,000)	22 (36.67)	16 (33.33)	22 (36.67)	20 (37.04)	44 (36.67)	36 (35.29)
High Income group 20,000 & above	11 (18.33)	11 (22.91)	24 (40)	23 (42.59)	35 (29.17)	34 (33.33)
Total	60 (100)	48 (100)	60 (100)	54 (100)	120	102

Source: Field Survey

From the above it is clear that 34.16% of differently abled belong to the low income group 36.67%belong to the middle income group and 29.17% belong to the high income group.

Classification according to the employment status of the differently abled and non-differently abled

Following table shows the employment status of the differently abled and non-differently abled:

Table 2 Employment Status

Employment Status	No. of rural respondents		No. of urban respondents	
	Differently abled	Non-differently abled	Different ly abled	Non-differently abled
Employed	18 (30)	29 (60.4)	22 (36.67)	31 (57.41)
Unemployed	42 (70)	19 (39.6)	38 (63.33)	23 (42.59)
Total	60(100)	48 (100)	60 (100)	54(100)

Source: Field Survey

From the above table it is clear that employment status of differently abled is worse compared to the non-differently abled category.

Classification according to the educational status of the differently abled and non-differently abled

Table below shows the educational status of the differently abled and non-differently abled.

Table 3 Educational Status

Educational Status	No. of rural respondents		No. of urban respondents	
	Differently abled	Non-differently abled	Differently abled	Non-differently abled
Educated	29	48	41	54
Uneducated	31	-	19	-
Total	60	48	60	54

Source: Field Survey

From the above analysis, it is clear that there are 31 uneducated differently abled in rural area and 19 in urban area. No one is uneducated while considering the non-differently abled category. From the above analysis it is clear that differently abled women have low income, employment and educational status compared to that of non-differently abled women. The situation is worse while we have a rural-urban comparison.

Empowerment of Differently abled Awareness about PWD Act and other legislations

The following table shows awareness about the PWD Act and other legislations.

Table 4 Awareness about PWD Act and other legislations

Awareness about PWD Act& other legislations	No. of rural respondents	No. of urban respondents	Total
Aware	4 (6.67)	9 (15)	13 (10.83)
Not Aware	56 (93.33)	51 (85)	107 (89.17)
Total	60 (100)	60 (100)	120 (100)

Source: Primary Survey

Above analysis depicted that 89.17% of differently abled women are not aware of PWD Act and other legislations.

Awareness of Possibilities of aids, appliances and stipends from LSG, NGO's or other government Institutions

Table shows awareness of possibilities of aids, appliances and stipends from LSG, NGO's or other government Institutions.

Table 5 Awareness of Possibilities of aids, appliances and stipends from LSG, NGO's or other government Institutions

Opinion	No. of rural respondents	No. of urban respondents	Total
Not aware	3 (5)	1 (1.67)	4 (3.33)
Aware only	6 (10)	9 (15)	15 (12.5)
Benefited	39 (65)	43 (71.66)	82 (68.34)
Denied	12 (20)	7 (11.67)	19 (15.83)
Total	60 (100)	60 (100)	120 (100)

Source: Primary Source

From above analysis it is clear that only 68.34% is benefited and nearly 15.83% are denied.

Benefits from different Government Bodies

Table below shows benefits from different governmental bodies such as gramapanchayat, Block Panchayat, District Panchayat, Co-operation, State Government and Central Government.

Table 6 Benefits from different Government Bodies

Institutions	No. of rural respondents	No. of urban respondents
Grama Panchayat	28 (71.8)	-
Block Panchayat	11 (28.21)	-
District Panchayat	4 (12.9)	-
Corporation	-	33 (76.74)
State Government	2 (5.13)	6 (13.95)
Central Government	-	2 (4.65)

Source: Field Survey

From the above table analysis it is clear that 71.8% got benefits from panchayat, at the same time 76.74% got benefit from co-operation and 8 women got benefit from state government while considering 39 beneficiaries from rural and 43 from urban.

Type of benefits or Concessions avail

Table shows type of benefits or concessions avail by the following Government programmes.

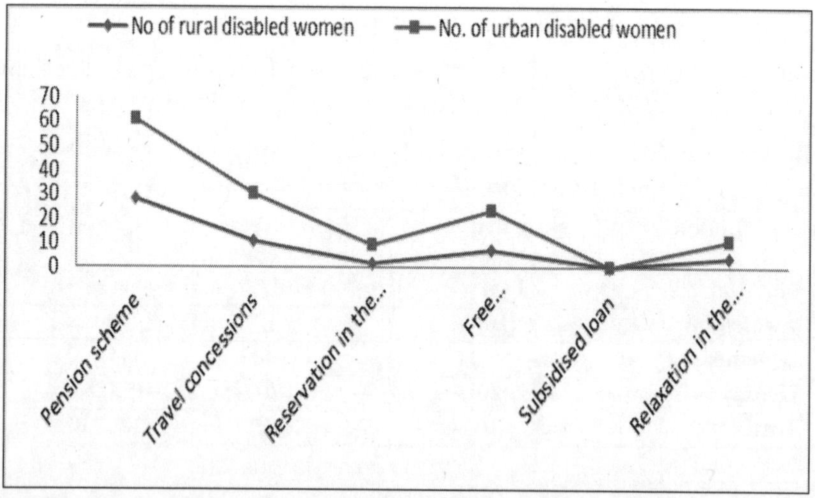

Fig 1 Type of benefits or Concessions avail

Source: Field Survey

From the above graph it is clear that most of them are benefitted with pension schemes. (out of 39 beneficiaries and one get 3 type of benefit. Out of 43 beneficiaries, 25 get 2 type of benefits and 7 get 3 type of benefits).

Type of Appliances received by the differently abled

Below table shows type of appliances received by the differently abled.

Table 7 Type of Appliances received by the differently abled

Type of Appliances	No. of rural respondents	No. of urban respondents	Total
Artificial limbs	-	-	-
Pair of crutches	2	4	6
Pair of surgical boots	2	4	6
Calipers	3	3	6
Calipers with crutches	-	3	3
Wheel chair	1	-	1
Auto cycle	-	-	-
Splint	-	-	-
Hearing aid	2	3	5
Visual aid	1	2	3
Alarm stick	-	-	-
Total	11	19	30

Source: Field Survey

From the above analysis it is clear that 11 differently abled in rural area and 19 in urban area received appliances.

Mode of appliances distribution

Following table shows the mode of distribution of appliances.

Table 8 Mode of appliances distribution

Mode of distribution	No. of rural respondents	No. of urban respondents	Total
Purchased	2 (18.18)	8 (42.11)	10 (33.33)
Issued free by Government Institutions	8 (72.73)	7 (36.84)	15 (50)
Gifted by NGOs	1 (9.09)	4 (21.05)	5 (16.67)
Total	11	19	30

Source: Field Survey

From the above analysis, it is clear that 50% of appliances are issued free by government institutions. Also 33.33% of appliances are purchased by themselves.

Following tables shows various needs and opinions of the differently abled women in Thiruvananthapuram District for their social integration and empowerment.

Need of Financial Assistance from Government

Table below shows priority of various needs of financial assistance from government.

Table 9 Need of Financial Assistance from Government

Opinion	No. of rural respondents	No. of urban respondents	Total
Financial assistance for self-employment	12 (20)	18 (30)	30 (25)
Financial assistance for marriage and children's marriage	8 (13.33)	4 (6.67)	12 (10)
Financial assistance from government for medical treatment and appliances	13 (21.67)	8 (13.33)	21 (17.5)
Disability Pension	20 (33.33)	14 (23.33)	34 (28.33)
Loan facility from bank as subsidy	7 (11.67)	16 (26.67)	23 (19.77)
Total	60 (100)	60 (100)	120 (100)

Source: Primary Survey

From above analysis it is clear that 33.33% need disability pension in rural area and in urban area 30% need financial assistance for self-employment.

Need of appliances from government

Table shows priority of various needs of appliances from government.

Table 10 Need of appliances from government

Need of Appliances	No. of rural respondents	No. of urban respondents	Total
Free distribution	36 (60)	21 (35)	57 (47.5)
Modern and new Technologies	13 (21.67)	24 (40)	37 (30.83)

Availabilities of all types of appliances in same area or market	11 (18.33)	15 (25)	26 (21.67)
Total	60 (100)	60 (100)	120 (100)

Source: Primary Source

Above analysis depicted that 60% opined free distribution of appliances in rural areas while 40% in urban area demand modern and new technologies.

Need for medical intervention

Table below shows priority in the need for medical intervention.

Table 11 Need for medical intervention

Need for medical intervention	No. of rural respondents	No. of urban respondents	Total
Resource mobilisation	6 (10)	16 (26.67)	22 (18.33)
Extension of Services to medical aid	2 (3.33)	8 (13.33)	10 (8.33)
Financial support from government	20 (33.33)	17 (28.33)	37 (30.83)
Proper medical treatments from hospital	14 (23.33)	13 (21.67)	27 (22.5)
Free medical facilities	18 (30)	6 (10)	24 (20)
Total	60 (100)	60 (100)	120 (100)

Source: Primary Survey

From above analysis it is clear that 33.33% from rural area and 28.33% from when area need financial support from government as medical intervention.

Need of Training

Table shows priority of various needs of training among the differently abled women

Table 12 Need of Training

Need of Training	No. of rural respondents	No. of urban respondents	Total
Job oriented and gainful training	21 (35)	18 (30)	39 (32.5)
Engineering or technological	11 (18.33)	20 (33.33)	31 (25.83)

training			
Entrepreneurship development programs	28 (46.67)	22 (36.67)	50 (41.67)
Total	60 (100)	60 (100)	120 (100)

Source: Primary Survey

From above analysis it is clear that most of them demand entrepreneurship development programmes as need of training.

Table 13 Need of Social Behaviour or Attitudinal change

Need of Social behavior or attitude change	No. of rural respondents	No. of urban respondents	Total
Community awareness	12 (20)	9 (15)	21 (17.5)
Social mobilisation	7 (11.66)	8 (13.33)	15 (12.5)
Counseling and guidance	14 (23.33)	10 (16.67)	24 (20)
Healthy interaction	7 (11.67)	15 (25)	22 (18.34)
Graceful Behaviour	7 (11.67)	12 (20)	19 (15.83)
Positive and constructive attitudes	13 (21.67)	6 (10)	19 (15.83)
Total	60 (100)	60 (100)	120 (100)

Source: Primary Source

From above analysis, it is clear that 20% demand counselling and guidance and 18.34% need healthy interaction of the society with them.

Conclusion

Government of India along with various departments provides lot of legislations, empowerment programmes and policy interventions for the well-being and inclusion of the most marginalised strata of society. All programmes are introduced to cater various needs and aspirations of this chunk of population. But in spite of all these programmes and policy interventions, largenumbers of differently abled people areoutliers because of the faulty implementation and lack of awareness among them since the education and work participation rate is low. Some programmes are not fully implemented and do not cover the entire differently abled population and some lack expert personnel, modern medical facilities, sophisticated aids and appliances etc. Also specific gender biased programmes for differently abled women who faces double discrimination in every walk of life is negligible. All these problems and limitations should be solved to integrate them to the mainstream of development. Dissemination of information and awareness generation is needed for prevention and early detection of disabilities in rural and urban areas. Empowerment is not the responsibility of Government or a few NGO's. It is the collective responsibility of the society. The fact we must recognise is that they are not disabled people but differently abled people and the catch word today is empathy not sympathy.

References

Barik, S. (2009). *Differently abled in India.* New Delhi: Adhyayan Publishers and Distributors

Deegan, Patricia. (1988). "Recovery: The Lived Experience of Empowerment" in *Psychosocial Empowerment Journal,* 11(4), 11-19.

Government of India. (2011). *Census of India 2011.* New Delhi: Registrar General and Census Commissioner.

Govt. of India. (2001). *National Human Development Report.* New Delhi: Planning Commission.

Information and Guidance booklet for Persons with Disabilities (2003). New Delhi: Empowerment Council of India

Rao, L. Govinda. (2004). *Biwako millennium framework for action-A guide for future in Mohapatra,* C.S(ed.) Disability Management in India, Challenges and Commitments. Secunderabad: NIMH.

Sunder, S. (2010). *Textbook of Empowerment.* New Delhi: Jaypee Brothers Medical Publishers (P) Ltd.

Sunder, S. (2010). *Textbook of Empowerment.* New Delhi: Jaypee Brothers Medical Publishers (P) Ltd.

The Government of India. (1992) *Empowerment Council of India Act.* New Delhi: Ministry of Social Justice and Empowerment.

The Government of India. (1995) *Persons with Disabilities (Equal Opportunities, Protection of Rights and Full Participation) Act.* New Delhi: Ministry of Social Justice and Empowerment.

The Government of India. (1999) *National Trust for Welfare of Persons with autism, cerebral palsy, mental retardation and Multiple Disability Act.* New Delhi: Ministry of Social Justice and Empowerment.

Walia, Gagandeep Kaur. (2014). *Disability in South Asia Network for Chronic Disease.* Retrieved June19, 2015,from http://docslide.us/documents/disability.html

WHO (2006). *WHO-Aims Report on Mental Health System in Uttarakhand, India.* Retrieved August 20, 2011 from http://www.searo.who.int/LinkFiles/Mental Health Resources WHO

World Report on Disability, 2011. *Geneva.* World Health Organisation.

2

Responsible Tourism in Kumarakom, Kerala: A Study on The Impact on The Responsibility and Quality of Life of Destination

Dr. Hari krishnan PK

Introduction

Tourism acts as a persuasive tool in assimilating the world into a global village, enabling the apportionment of resources from the generating economies to the developing ones. It is recognised as one of the fastest growing industries in the world, which gives it a prime role in the future world's economy and employment. Tourism to developing countries has augmented, making it a vital component of economic development in countries with exotic wildlife, scenery, beaches, shopping, culture or even sex (Knox PL &, Marston SA, 2007).

Kumara kommodel of Responsible tourism

In Kerala although tourism is perceived and promoted as a 'development paradigm' and a tool for economic and employment growth, factors like the rate of leakage of tourism inward receipts and to what extent the local economy retains the revenues generated by tourism is not clear. An analysis of this has helped to establish baseline data on the local linkages, and a measurable road map to surge local benefits. Thus Responsible tourism was conceived as a game changer which can be developed through democratisation involving local self-governments and stake holders. This involved creating arenas of meaningful dialogue and policy-making for responsibility of the destination.

A protuberant trail towards this, is to constitutionally empower local governments as primary decision-makers on matters regarding tourism development of that area. The formation of stakeholder Committee on Tourism at Kumarakom as per section 163(1) of the Kerala Panchayat Raj Act was a significant step towards responsible tourism whereby local self-government becoming primary stake holders in decision making through a democratic and consultative process. This policy conceived through democratisation process formalised by local self-governments become an effective tool for change. This process evolved into tourism products / services of that destination is the outcome of this. Based on this, Department of Tourism, Govt, of Kerala declared Kumarakom as one of the pilot Responsible destinations in 2007.

The initial aim was to identify new zones or unexplored destinations which have a tremendous tourism potential and turning them to a responsible destination with the active participation of the local community. This will safeguard the rights of the local community, preserve the ecological and cultural fabric of a destination and ensure its holistic development. Gramasabhas (village communities) will be formed in each destination and have a major role in framing destination specific tourism policies.

Kumarakom is a model destination built on the tenants of public/private synergy in tourism that works towards responsible tourism objectives. The Kumarakom responsible practices has positively impacted more than 1.000 members of the local community across the tourism value chain. The Kumarakom responsible initiative in Kerala is therefore an ideal illustration to analyse how a destination can be turned as ideal destination for local empowerment of host community and enhanced visitor experience thereby augmenting economy, sustain environment and social and cultural preservation

Enhancing Local Economy

The first initiative was to enhance the economic development of local population through the activities which will enable the community to harness the novel steps and take proactive role for rolling out this scheme. Linkage between hotels/resorts and the local farmers was established whereby they agreed to procure vegetable, local fruits from the local producers only.

Conserving culture and Preserving arts

After that local cultural and artistic groups were identified and linkage was established with hotels and resorts for daily performance during tourist season. This has benefited the local artists to earn additional income and also for the revival and preservation of traditional art forms of Kerala.

Local Entrepreneurship Promotion

Following this an initiative was launched to identify skilled handicrafts and give skill training to develop local souvenirs. These locally crafted souvenirs were marketed by the tour operators and hotel and resorts in the area thereby providing employment and income to the local community. Self Help Groups (SHG) of women started an ethnic cuisine restaurant in Kumarakom serving locally flavoured dishes at reasonable price. Other groups also ventured in to products which can be procured by the local hotels like paper and cloth bags, brooms, coir mats, candle lights, curry powders and perishable products like milk, vegetables, pickles, floral arrangements and flour.

Showcasing local and social experiences as products (Village Life Experiences (VLE))

These ingenious holiday packages showcasing the rural life, culture and occupation of the destination is a form of social interaction for the visitors. This include visit to local fish, duck, vegetable, paddy farms, and local activities including toddy tapping, coconut leaf weaving, coir making, coconut climbing, toddy tapping, broom stick making, screw pine weaving traditional bow and arrow fishing. Thus tourism in Kumarakom has become an evocative social experience for the visited and visitors.

Generation of Local employment

The rolling out of Responsible tourism has helped women empowerment and better the status of local women by the way of entrepreneurship and employment. Women entrepreneurs have been instrumental in making substantial growth in their income through Agro ventures and employment in hotels and resorts. Large number of women were given skill training to get employed in gardening, kitchen, house-keeping etc. (Dr. B. Vijaya Kumar, Rupesh kumar K,

Saroop Roy, 2013). Men were employed as boat crew, chauffeurs, electricians, plumbers, housekeeping staff in various accommodation units.

Environmental preservation

The responsible tourism practice in Kumarakom also embarked a responsible environment protection and waste free destination drive through "Clean Vembanad Initiative". Synergy of houseboat owners, enterprises, employees etc. continuously cleared the houseboat waste and entrusted a society for plastic waste collection

Conclusion

The highly successful, must-emulate Kumarakom model of Responsible tourism destination development is the outcome of local leadership, community acceptance, industry initiative and visitor responsiveness. As they vary from one geographical area to another these are by no means the only decisive factors for the success of modelling. Bringing Responsibility in tourism cannot be a one-time process but one that is incessant and evolving dynamically due to the involvement and integration of all stakeholders who get enriched and will be affected by tourism development.

The key for successful execution and upscaling of these principles is to involve all stakeholders of tourism such as local self-governments and host communities, governmental Departments of Tourism, environment & forests, commerce & industry, women & child and local self-government, representatives from, tourism industry, advocacy groups so that they all have a role to play in evolving local tourism policy planning. This phenomena poses a challenge to all stakeholders and they have to face the challenge. They must review not only exterior influences and policies but also restructure and revise their own internal systems to direct tourism development towards responsibility.

References

Ashley, Meyer, D., Page, S., & Roe, D. (2004). *Tourism and the Poor: Analysing and Interpreting Toutism Statistics from a Poverty Perspective.* London : PPT Partnership.

Department of Tourism, g. o. (2018). *Kumarakom Destination Units Income-2017 April To 2018 March.* Retrieved from www.keralatourism.org/responsible-tourism.

Dr. B. Vijaya Kumar, Rupesh kumar K, Saroop Roy. (2013). *Resposible Tourism Initiative of Kerala.* A Case Study of kumarakom. KITTS.

Goodwin, H. (2011). *Taking Responsibility for Tourism.* Goodfellow Publishers limited.

Knox PL &, Marston SA. (2007). *Human Geography, Places and Regions in Global Context.* Pearson Education Ltd.

Neto, F. (2003). "A new approach to responsible tourism development: moving beyond environmental protection." *Natural REsources Forum, 27*, 210-223.

Responsible Development of Tourism. (2014). *International Forum on Responsible Development of Tourism & Innovation.*

Swarbrooke. (1999). *Responsible Tourism management.* CABI.

Tourism, M. o. (2002). *National Tourism Policy 2002.* Ministry of Tourism.

UNWTO. (1993). *http://sdt.unwto.org/content/about-us-5.* Retrieved from UNWTO: http://sdt.unwto.org

UNWTO, UNEP. (2005). *Making Tourism more Responsible, A Guide for Policy Makers.* UNWTO, UNEP.

WTTC. (2018). *Travel and Tourism Economic Impact 2018 World.* WTTC. Retrieved from www.wttc.org

3

Beach Tourism in Kanyakumari District

Dr. D. Lekha

Introduction

Kanyakumari District, southern most tip of the Indian sub-continent, get its name from the township Kanyakumari, a pilgrim centre associated with the temple of Goddess Kanyakumari The District was part of Travancore Princely state during the pre-independence period, after the independence it remained a part of Travancore-Cochin state until the realignment of linguistic basis was achieved. The headquarters of Kanyakumari District is Nagercoil. There are many places of interest for the domestic and foreign tourists. The traditional areas of tourist attractions like beaches, religious places, historical monuments and cultural attractions continue to attract millions of visitors.

Kanyakumari District has breathtaking beautiful beaches. The swaying coconut palms and the sand add to the holiday mood. Take a plunge into swimming the most relaxing water activity that can be pursued here. The sun bathing is also another attraction for the sun starved tourists. The beaches here are the right place for fun and frolic either a family holiday or a tour excursion.[1] Amongst the popular beaches of Kanyakumari District are Kanyakumari beach, Vattakottai beach, Chotthavilai beach, Muttom beach and Thengapattinam beach.

Kanyakumari Beach

By its very location, Kanyakumari occupies a unique place among the tourist centers of India. It has a fine beach landscape with sands of myriad colour.[2] From the beautiful beach, one can simultaneously witness the glorious sight of the moon rising up in the east and sun setting in the west, on a full moon day. Kanyakumari is the southern most tip of the Indian peninsula, where the Arabian Sea, the Indian Ocean and the Bay of Bengal confluence. It is a rare scene in the world. A dip in the confluence point of the three Seas is considered holy. There is also *in this place also a health resort* and a picnic spot. There is a bathing ghat, where the pilgrims take bath on holy days.[3] This place has been associated with great men like Swami Vivekananda and Mahatma Gandhi in whose names memorials have been built here. They are beautiful and add to the attraction of this place. The beautiful Gandhi Memorial completed in 1956 is situated as a memorial to the Father of the Nation. An urn of Mahatma Gandhi was kept here for public to pay homage before immersion.[4]

Vattakottai Beach

Vatakottai, a granite fort six kilometers north-east of Kanyakumari forms the terminal of a line of ramparts known as the South Travancore line, built by Marthanda Varma to serve as defense for Nanjil Nadu. Adjacent to the Vattakottai fort, there is a beautiful beach. From the fort it gives a very good view of the sea. The beach is a very good place to spend the evening with family and friends.[5]

Chotthavilai Beach

This beach is about 10 kms from Kanyakumari and one of the best natural beaches of the district. The beach has shallow water and high sand dunes on the back ground. There are rest shelters, huts and a view tower over here for the benefit of tourists. The tourists can reach the beach through the newly laid costal road which is a very beautiful drive along the sea-coast.[6]

Sanguthurai Beach

Sanguthurai is a beautiful beach resort and is very convenient for the local population of Nagercoil. It is only about 10 kms from the town. A children's park, seating facility, open huts with Terracotta roofs and lighting facilities are available.[7]

Colachel

The sea coast town is situated about 22 kms west of Nagercoil. It was a port of call for European Merchants during the 16-18th Centuries. The Dutch and the English had their trading settlements here. This place has afforded natural amenities for shipping by its physiographical structure, a group of outlying rocks forming a practical break water. Under cover of these rocks are done loading and unloading and other shipping operations. A variety of commodities is exported from here.[8]

Muttom Beach

The famous beach at Muttom is located about 32 kms from Kanyakumari. Muttom is delightful place on the coast of Kalkulam taluk, attracting people desirous of having a seaside holiday. From the inscriptions belonging to the 18th year of the great Chola King, Raja Raja I, found in the rock cut cave temple at Thirunandhikarai. It is learnt that he captured Muttom and renamed it as Mummudi Chola Nallur.[9] This beach is famous for its beautiful landscaping and high rocks dipping into the sea at the beach side. The sun set view point at Muttom is one of the most panoramic view points in the district. Another attraction of Muttom is the century old light-house built by the British. However so far this beautiful beach has always been unsafe for the tourists since the rocks on which tourists go to see the sea view are slippery and a number of fatal accidents have occurred over the past few years. Protective stainless steel fencing is established across the entire dangerous areas.[10]

Thikkurichi Beach

It is located near Rajakkamangalam Thurai. The amazing Arabian sea, the golden glowing sands and the coconut canopies all come together as a package for the picture perfect holiday. A swim or bath here is rejuvenation and relaxation for the tourists. Here feel the cool breeze of the wondrous waves.[11]

Thengapattinam Beach

It is another beautiful beach of Kanyakumari district. It is 35 kms from Nagercoil. As coconuts are abundant in this place this might have derived this name. This place had in ancient times, trade relations with foreign countries like Arabia. There was direct cargo boat service between Thengapattinam and other foreign maritime towns. Copra, dry fish, coir and sharkfin were the main products that were exported. It is very good place for water sports and other aqua tourism activities.[12]

Conclusion

The major tourist generating countries to Kanyakumari district are U.K, U.S.A, Sri Lanka, France, Germany, Japan, Italy, Malaysia, Canada, Australia and Singapore. Coastal and beach tourism remains as the major motivator to Kanyakumari District. Sustainable Tourism has to provide for intergenerational equity with equitable distribution of the costs and benefits of tourism development occurring among both present and future generation.

End Notes

1. Gopalakrishnan (ed), Kanyakumari District Gazetteer
2. S. Padmanabhan, Temples in Kanyakumari District P. 130
3. Vision 2020, Kanyakumari KRRC, Nagercoil P. 208
4. The Tale of Vivekananda Rock Memorial, Kanyakumari, Vivekananda Kendra P 50
5. Census of India, 1981, Kanyakumari District Part XIII A & B P. 15
6. Vision 2020: op cit P209
7. Ibid
8. V. Nagam Aiya, *Travancore State Manuel*, Travancore Vol III P. 575
9. S. Padmanabhan, the Forgotten History of the Lands End P. 5
10. Note from the Director of Light House and Light ships, Madras dated 23 July 1986
11. S. Padmanabhan, The Contribution of Kanyakumari 1987 Nagercoil, Kumari Press P 10
12. Report from the Collector of Kanyakumari dated 28 Oct 1987.

4

A Study on Savitribai Phule, Pioneer of Dalit Women Liberation in India

Dr.V. Santhiya

Introduction

The situation of Dalit women needs special attention. Dalit women are one of the largest socially segregated groups anywhere in the world. Although both Dalit men and women suffer under the same traditional taboos, Dalit women are confronted with these more often. They are discriminated against not only by the people of higher castes, but also within their own communities, where men are dominant.

Paul Divakar, one of the founders of the national campaign on Dalit Human Rights expressed the need to fight for the human rights of Dalit women. Though the ages, Dalit women continued to be illiterate, malnourished, in poor health, over worked, oppressed and victimised by a number of factors, including their own family and community.

The present Maharashtra state played a crucial role in the socio, political and religious movements during the past. Innumerable number of personalities emerged in this region for the cause of women liberation. The most important notable personality who sacrificed his entire life for the cause of Dalit emancipation was Jyothiba Phule. He was called as Mahatma prior to Mohandas Karamchand Gandhi. His beloved wife was Savitribai Phule who also did a creditable role for the liberation of Dalit women and also laid the foundation for the educational development of the so called depressed class people of that region.

Early Life

Savitribai Phule was a social reformer, emancipator of women and angel of Dalit women liberation movement in India. She was the wife of Jothiba Phule, the first Indian who was called as Mahatma. She was born on 3rd January 1831 in a wealthy farmer's family at a small village Naigaum of Satara District in Maharastra State. Savitribai was married at a very tender age of 9. Jyothiba Phule, the social reformer needed some female teachers to help him in achieving his goal. Thus he taught and trained his wife as a role model teacher. Gradually the news reached his father who threatened to drive him out of his house due to the fear of possible attack from orthodox elements. When the choice before Savitribai Phule was either going away with her husband or staying back with her in-laws. She preferred to be with her husband. After that Jothiba Phule sent her to a training school where she passed out in flying colours and became the first Indian female teacher. Significantly she joined in the first girl's school started by her husband. Savitribai was a poet also who is considered as a pioneer of Marathi poetry.

Mother of Women Education

Savitribai Phule opened a school in Pune for girls in the year 1848 at Bhideswada. Initially nine girls enrolled themselves as students and they belonged to different castes. Savitribai Phule used to leave for the school early in the morning. The contemporary orthodox society was not prepared for this "misadventure" as women's education failed to get significance.

Savitribai Phule continued teaching the girls despite all opposition from the society. She was even abused by the orthodox society. She lost all her courage after facing such ill-treatments and even decided to give up her job also. But her husband constantly supported her and encouraged to continue with her efforts. In spite of the entire ordeals, Savitribai continued her teaching slowly and gradually. Because of the efforts, the school played a crucial role in preventing and diminishing violence in the classroom and in all aspects of the school. It gave positive reinforcement to appropriate behaviour. Significantly Phule's family was honoured by the British Government for their outstanding contribution in the field of education and Savitribai was honoured with the best teacher award on the 16th November 1852.

Savitribai Phule and Widow Remarriage

Savitribai Phule realised that along with education it was necessary to work on other social fronts like to build-up self esteem and confidence of women. She also campaigned against some cruel social practices. Many girls who got married at the young age turned widows at the early age particularly before twelve-thriteen. After the death of their husbands either they would have to take sati (a practice of self-immolation by the widow on the funeral pyre of the husband) or their head would be clean shaved to make them ugly and unattractive to other men. These unfortunate helpless women were denied their basic rights like men.

The resultant pregnant widows would be scared of being ostracised by the society like the child would have to suffer and would resort to suicide or killing the newborn. To counteract this situation, Jyotirao and Savitribai started a home for the pregnant widows and orphaned children to stop this disaster. Savitribai had run the home capably. She considered all the children in the orphanage as her own. Savitribai and Jyotirao were moved by the plights of such widows and castigated the barbers. They organised a strike of barbers and persuaded them not to shave the heads of widows. This was the first strike of its kind.

Savitribai Phule and Other Social Reforms

Savitribai Phule was not only involved in the educational activities of Jyotirao, but also in all the social agitations that he launched. They also fought against all forms of social prejudices. They were moved to see the untouchables who were refused to use the drinking water meant for the upper castes. Both Jyotirao and Savitribai opened up their reservoir of water to the so called untouchables in the precincts of their house.

Once Jyotirao and Savitribai stopped a pregnant lady from suicide, promising her to give her child his name after it was born. Savitribai readily accepted the lady in her house and willingly assured to help her to deliver the child. Savitribai later on adopted this child who then grew up to become a doctor. This incident opened new horizons for the couple. Many women were driven to commit suicide by men who had exploited them to satisfy their lust and then deserted them. Therefore Savitribai Phule put boards on streets about the "Delivery home" for pregnant women. The delivery home was called "Balhatya Pratibandhak Griba".

Savitribai opposed idolatry and questioned the rationale of such practice. She faced social isolation and vicious attacks from the people whom she questioned. After the demise of Jyothibai Phule,

Savitribai took over the responsibility of Satya Shodhak Samaj, which was founded by her husband. She presided over meetings and guided workers. In 1868 she welcomed the so called untouchables to take water from her bore well. Savitribai Phule started Mahila Seva Mandal in 1852 which worked for raising women's consciousness on their human rights. Another notable achievement was the inauguration of infanticide prohibition home on 28th January 1853 in order to check female infanticide.

Conclusion

Savitribai Phule was the first women teacher of India. She was the first women educationist, the first poet and the foremost emancipator of women in India. Savitribai Phule passed away on the 10th March 1897. Savitribai's poems and other writings are still an inspiration to others. Two of her books were published by Kavya Phule and Bavan Kashi Subodh Ratnakar respectively. Recently the Maharashtra Government started a special award in her name for women who work for social causes. On the occasion of her birth anniversary, a commemorative stamp was released by the Department of Post and Telegraph, Government of India on March 10, 1998 in order to honour Savitribai's contribution to the Indian society particularly Dalit women.

Eventhough Savitribai Phule worked for the removal of violence against women, the women folk in India in general faces innumerable problems even now, So preventing violence will require sustained violence will require sustained and systematic efforts, by students, teachers and schools, and more widely, in families communities and nations. Then only Savitribai Phule's soul will get rest in peace.

References

P.G. Patil, Collected works of Mahatma Jotirao Phule, Vol. II, Published by Education department, Govt. of Maharashtra.

Kamala Ganesh & Usha Thakkar, Culture and the making of identity in contemporary India.

P.K. Ravindranath, Sharad Pawar the making of a Modern Maharashtra.

Nisar, M. Kandaswamy, Meena, Ayyankali – Dalit Leader of Organic Protest.

"It's Savitribai Phule University", Time of India, Retrieved 7th August, 2014.

S.G. Mahajan, Pune City, its History Growth and Development (1758 to 1988 A.D.)

5

Ric Perspectives of Khadar Development Programmes of Rajajiin Madras Presidency

Dr. S. Doral

Introduction

Khadar is not only an-apparent apparel but also a thing is woven with national spirit and Self-respect. During the independence Struggle in India Khadar was a symbol of Swaraj. The movement of Khadar would look strange to the people who belong to the present generation and who do not know the history of the freedom struggle in India. C.R.Das an eminent Congress leader and freedom fighter regarding Khadar says: "We must regard Khaddar (Khadar) as a symbol of Swaraj. As the Khadar makes us self-contained about a very large department of our national life so it is hoped that the inspiration of Khaddar will make the whole of our national life self-contained and independent. This is the meaning of the symbol. To my mind, such symbol worship requires the spreading out of all non-co-operation activities in every possible direction. It is thus and only thus that speedy attainment of Swaraj is possible".

Development of Khadi Programme

Regarding the importance of Khadar, Mahatma Gandhi says, "Britain's chief interest center around the Lancashire trade with India. It is one thing more than any other that had ruined the Indian peasant and imposed partial idleness upon him by depriving him of the one supplementary occupation he had. Boycott of foreign cloth is therefore a necessity if he is to live. The plan, therefore, is not merely to induce the peasant to refuse to buy the cheap and nice-looking foreign fabric but also by teaching him to utilise his spare hours in carding and spinning cotton and getting it woven by the village weavers to dress in Khaddar so woven and thus to save him the cost of buying foreign and for that matter even Indian mill-made cloth. Thus, the boycott of foreign using hand spinning and hand weaving i.e., Khadar, not only saves the peasant's families but it enables us, workers, to render special service of a first-class order. It brings us into direct touch with the village and it enables us to give them real political education and teach them to become self-reliant. The organisation of Khaddar is thus infinitely better than co-operative societies or any other form of village organisation". Khadi is considered only as a part-time job-off rainy season and full-time employment during the famine. But Gandhiji often said, "Without a Cottage Industry the Indian Peasant is Doomed. He cannot maintain himself from the produce of the land in its supplementary industry". In a letter dated February 15,1922, Gandhi wrote, "Of all my outward activities I do believe that the spinning wheel is the most permanent and the most beneficial. I have abundant proof now to support my statement that the spinning wheel will solve the problem of the economic distress in millions of Indian houses, and it constitutes effective insurance against famine". He further opined, "The spinning wheel is a foundation for all public co-operative life.

It is impossible to build any permanent public life without it. It is the one visible link that in dissolubly binds us to the lowest in the land and thus gives them hope". Following Gandhiji, Rajaji gave much more importance to the growth of the cottage industry than heavy industries. Rajaji was not against the development born of modernity on the other hand he wanted to maintain the labour-capital relationship in a conciliatory style to maintain an economy weighed in favour of Khadi and handloom industries. He laid more emphasis on developing small-scale industries than heavy industries and advocated the Khadi scheme. The object of the Khadi scheme was twofold, just to employ the unemployed and underemployed rural population, as spinning offered the simplest avocation in life. Secondly, it was to achieve self-sufficiency in cloth in terms of Khadi in the villages. He further believed that it was the only way by which the villages could be made self-sufficient economic units. As such he became an ardent follower of Gandhi in propagating Khadi. Rajaji took up the Khadi development programme as a measure of social progress. The growth of Textile mills made it difficult for the poor weavers to compete with mill products. The foreign competition had especially paralysed the spinning and weaving trades. The weaver stood helpless before the gigantic array of machines and machine-made clothes of mighty Manchester. The free trade principles applied to India brought about the complete ruin of this class of industry in South India Rajaji strongly believed that the Indian problem of hunger could be solved only by making people industrious and not by mere industrialisation. Khadi was an integral part of the original Swaraj programme of 1920. In1921-22 thousands of congressmen repeated from hundreds of platforms that Swaraj for the millions depended upon the spinning wheel humming in every village, Rajaji took up the Khadi development as part of the Congress Constructive Programme in the South in 1922. He rendered valuable service to the development of Khadi and Handloom even before coming to the power and it is evident from his introduction of the Khadi scheme at the Tiruchengcode Ashram in 1925. The long absence of rains in the year 1925 resulted in boosting the development of Khadi in and around the Ashram. The charka was the only alternative means of income. Plenty of yarn was produced for the use of weavers. Rajaji by his Khadi scheme not only gave employment to the poor but also made periodical appeals to them to save a little money every weak and not spend everything on drink, He also persuaded several mills in Tamil Nadu, not to produce thick yarn so that weavers would be obliged to accept hand spun he organised the south Indian Khadi Exhibition to remove the public criticism on it.

Growth of Handloom Industry

One of the first moves by the ministry was to allot rupees 2,00,000 for the encouragement of the handloom industry in the first budget. The Government extended necessary assistance that would enable the peasant families to supplement their income. A group of members with rural backgrounds contended that the budget had an urban bias and that allotment was inadequate to meet the needs of the handloom industry. The representatives of the commercial interests opposed it severely. Rajaji gave reason for his inclination to Khadi and Handloom industry. Such assistance for the effective renewal of a lost industry is a reasonable charge on the revenue of the province. The industry must be given some measure of assistance to enable it to be renewed and become again a source of supplementary income to a peasant family. Rajaji openly declared Let the Capitalist build up special Industries, but agriculture and cloth must be left untouched as common property, for they are the only assets for the poorer members of the nation. It was this idea in his mind that made him pass the Madras Regulation of Sale of Cloth Act, 1937.This Act made provision for a levy of rupees two per year in the case of merchants who had a turnover of rupees three thousand or less per month and rupees five a year for others. The system of licensing cloth dealers introduced by the Act provided for a levy of license fees on dealers in Mill Cloth as a measure of protection by exempting those dealing exclusively in Khadi and handloom products.

T. Krishnamacharia, a member of the Legislative Council pointed out the flaws in the Act. He ridiculed the idea of licensing cloth shops, stood against the imposition of such tax and requested the Government to show consideration to other industries also. B. Bhaktavatsala Naidu, a member of the Justice Party opposed it since it discriminated between mill cloth and handloom cloth. Mahmud Shamshad, a member of the Muslim League, also opposed the Act as it affected even the small merchant. Rajaji in his reply to those oppositions stated that if there was any group against whom the Act aimed it was the Indian and European-owned cotton weaving mills in Bombay and Ahmadabad, not the mills which produced almost entirely yarn, much of which was sold to hand-weavers in the Presidency. Even though this Act did not bring in considerable revenue, it served as a pacesetter for the later attempts to give protection to khadar and hand-woven cloth. Further, the Government sanctioned the expenditure incurred for hand spinning and the Khadi manufacture movement. It also sanctioned the payment of subsidies for the period 1937-1938. Moreover, it paid rupees three lakhs to the "All India Spinner's Association" for Khadi development. The grants were spent on distributing Charkas and establishing spinning centers in many of the famine-stricken areas of Madras state. The handloom products were also exempted from the general Sales Tax. Further, the handloom weavers have helped with up-to-date designs and the Government directed that the staff of the Textile Institute should be utilised for the purpose. The capitalist press and some Congress politicians condemned his textile policy continuously. But he stood firm like a rock and stated that to create a proper atmosphere for the development of Khadi his Government would not allow the establishment of any new textile mill in the province. Thus his Khadi scheme provided remunerative employment for the largely ruralagricultural population, especially during the off-season. It also proved to be a good famine relief measure during a time of distress. While Rajaji was taking all these measures in Madras Presidency, the Congress Working Committee in its Haripura Conference held on 24th February1938 passed the following resolution on Khadi: "This committee notes with satisfaction the policy adopted by the All India Spinners and other Artisans engaged in the production of Khadi and the steps taken by it in that behalf, and calls upon all Congressmen and the public, in general, to give full co-operation in making this policy success by purchasing only that Khadi which is certified by the All Indian Spinners Association.

Khadi and Handloom Development

When Rajaji became the Chief Minister of Madras Presidency in 1952 he once again took up the Khadi and handloom scheme seriously and also made recommendations to the Government of India. He asked, "The state provided no workshop no training centers and no educational facilities to handloom weavers, why there is a Research Development Department for the mills and not for the charka and the handloom. With this appeal to the public, his government framed its textile policy so that mills cannot kill handloom cloth or Khadi. His Khadi scheme was operated in two parts such as intensive and extensive. Under this scheme, charkas and other implements were supplied at cost price; the cost was recovered in installments. The very essential raw material cotton was supplied to spinners at the cost price itself. The centers selected were three in Tamil Nadu, viz., Avinasi, Vellakoil, Chinna Salem, one in Kerala, Payyanur and three in Andhra, Guruvareddipalayam, Kotauratla and Erragondapalayam. The immediate objective of the scheme was to arrange for the production of Khadi in each of the centers sufficient to make available to the local population supplies at the rate of twenty yards for adults and ten yards for a child per annum. It was proposed to achieve this by securing at least one efficient spinner from each family residing in the center. Provision was made for supplying charkas to new spinners at a cost price. The spinners were encouraged to grow their cotton to make them self-sufficient in respect of cotton in the centers and supply to the spinners at a cost price.

The authorities in charge of these schemes were asked to take steps to increase the weaving capacity of each village so that the yarn spun in the village was woven into cloth in that village itself. The central Khadi committees and village Khadi committees constituted under the scheme were asked to carry the propaganda to the centers to create public opinion in favour of Khadi and also to exhibit the necessary spinner by the house-to-house propaganda. A paid staff was also appointed to assist the committee in their work. Though in the beginning it was expected that the Khadi produced in the center would be consumed by the local population later it was decided that all Government Departments should use Khadi only. The Government took such measure with a view that the use of Khadi would have a unifying influence and would be the best expression of homage to the memory of Gandhiji. This scheme was extended to several Firkas and worked successfully under the supervision of Rural Welfare Officers assisted by Khadi workers and Gram sevakas. With the merger of the rural welfare in the National Extensive service in October 1953, the working of the scheme was entrusted to the Block Development Officers-in-charge of the National Extensive Service block of the respective Firkas. The extensive Khadi scheme was introduced in the first instance in 19selected Firkas. This scheme provided for the introduction of thousand charkas a year in each of the 19 selected Firkas. The arrangements were made for supplying charkas at a concessional price and for the supply of cotton and instruments. The subsidy was also paid to self-spinner. The intention was that the extensive Khadi scheme should pave the way for the introduction of the Intensive Khadi scheme in due course. The total expenditure to the Government during the year 1953-54 on the intensive and extensive parts was rupees 16,68,113 – while the total income by the sale of cloth and cotton during the year was rupees 12,90,268. The Government also created the Khadi and Village Industries Board with the Minister of Agriculture as Chairman and

The Director of Rural Welfare as Secretary to advise the Government on matters relating to the development of Khadi and Handloom industries. Along with Khadi, Rajaji tried to encourage Handloom Industry also. A state Handloom Committee was formed to advise the State Government on all matters relating to the development of the Handloom Industry. In the districts, District Handloom Boards under the chairmanship of Collectors were constituted to advise the collectors on local problems relating to the Handloom Industry. The proposal for establishing Statutory Handloom Board was dropped on the ground that it would do more harm than good to handloom weavers. Hence the creation of a separate Handloom Department was given up. However, the Government undertook Relief Scheme to meet the great slump in the handloom industry that began in March 1952 and continued till the end of 1953. The State Handloom Committee recommended to the Government that no more power loom should be permitted to be installed in the province. With the help of the Yarn Advisory Committee, ration cards were issued and the yarn was distributed based on the active looms. To protect the handloom industry, the Government of India reserved certain varieties of cotton fabrics for production by that industry alone. When the yarn supply position became easy, the distribution of yarn on the card system was suspended. An International Marketing Scheme was undertaken in the middle of 1953. The Government of India passed the Central Act called the Khadi and other Handloom Industries Development Act, 1953 and relaxed yarn and cloth controls. Thereafter the production increased from rupees 18 lakhs per month to rupees 60lakhs per month and the sale increased from rupees 21 lakhs per month to rupees 60 lakhs per month. The socio-economic conditions of the handloom weavers improved considerably and they looked forward to an era of development during the period of the second five-year plan. Rajaji also appealed to the people to co-operate and patronize Khadi and Handloom cloth wherever it might be available and for every purpose for which it would be used in preference to mill cloth. Everyone must help the weak handloom weavers and their families from starvation.

People could make everything they wished out of handloom cloth, provided they paid a little attention. No subsidies or other help could come up to the help that the public could give. Ultimately any subsidy could help only when the public would come and buy handloom cloth. When people decided to buy this decent and durable cloth the life of a handloom weaver would no longer be unhappy. Rajaji remarked, “One out of every twelve families in our state was a weaving family that desired to maintain itself on honest labour”. Rajaji even pointed out that a self-respecting and self-supporting section of the population of the order of six million depended on the handloom industry and everyone must buy handloom cloth. During a press conference emphasized that the question of reservation of the manufacture of the dhotis and sarees to the handloom industry was not a question of yardage, but of human families whose care was the obligation of the State Government and therefore of the Central government. At this juncture, Rajaji recalled his past effort in that regard. "Seventeen Years ago I obtained from the Legislative Assembly of undivided Madras a unanimous resolution demanding that the union Governments would ban textile from producing bordered dhotis and coloured or printed sarees, leaving these items of production to the millions of handloom weavers who live on that cottage industry without throwing ally burden on Government".

Conclusion

As a result of Rajaji's efforts, Khadi and Handloom Industry made great and rapid progress. Today handloom industry occupies a very prominent in the state. This success has gone a long way to making villages economically self-sufficient and has thus helped rural uplift. In promoting the State's economic development Rajaji as an administrator provided the state first with a sound agricultural base so that progress in industries could follow up, once self-sufficiency in food was achieved. Thus, the rural development programmes of Rajaji brought tremendous changes in the socio-economic, life of the people of Madras Presidency. Thus his rural welfare schemes provided remunerative employment for the largely rural weaving population, especially during the off-season. It also proved to be a good famine relief measure during a time of distress.

Reference

Copley. A.R., *The Political Career of C. Rajagopalachari – A Moralist in Politics*, Bombay, 1978.

Rajayyan. K., *Early Tamilnadu*, Madras, 1984.

Chintamani. C.Y., (ed.), *Indian Social Reform Movement*, Part-I, Madras, 1901.

Gopalakrishna Gandhi, *Tamil Nadu District Gazetteer*, Pudukkotai, 1983.

RajaRaman, *Chennai through the Ages*, Chennai. 1997.

Boag. G.T., *Madras Presidency* 1881-1931, Madras. 1933.

Ramaswami. A., *Tamilnadu District Gazetteer*, Madras, 1972.

Saroja Sundara Rajan, *Madras Presidency in the Pre-Gardhian era A historic Perspective* 1884-1915, Pondicherry, 1977.

Murthy. R.K.., *Rajaji Life and Work*, Madras, 1979.

Madras State Administrative Report, 1937-38.

Baliga. B.S., *Studies in Madras Administration*, Vol.I and II, Madras, 1957.

Desai. A.R., *Social Background to Indian Nationalism*. New Delhi: Vikas, 1978.

Legislative Measures of Popular Ministries, Vol.I.

Rajmohan Gandhi, *TheRajaji Story 1937-1972*, Vo1.II. Bombay. 1984.

Report on the Administration of Madras State 1937-1938.

Narasimhachari. K.T., C.Rajagopalachari, *His Life and Mind*, New Delhi, 1978.

Panneer Selvam, *The Role of Rajaji in the Implementation of Congress Ideology in Tamil Nadu-A StudyIndian Historical Studies*, Tiruchirappalli, April 2009.

Rajagopalachari. C., *Khadhi Development in Madras State*, Madras, 1954.

Baliga. B.S., *History of Handloom Industry in Madras*, Government of Madras, 1960.

Madras Information, Vol. VI, No.10, October 1922.

6

The Social Renaissance of Kerala

Dr. Anand Lali Seena

Introduction

The 19th and 20th centuries witnessed the emergence of a new social order in Kerala under the impact of diverse social, economic and cultural influences. Even towards the end of 18th century the traditional social structure had begun to show signs of tottering. The centralising policies of Marthanda Varma and Sakthan Thampuran served to give the coup de grace to the old social order and ushered in before long a new era where in the feudal nobility and the caste aristocracy lost their old position of primacy. Even the Brahmins, Kshatriyas and upper castes came within the fold of this awakening and advocated radical social reform.

Social Structure of Kerala

Kerala Society was not based on the principles of social freedom and equality. The high castes like the Namboodiris, Kshatriyas and Nairs enjoyed several immunities and privileges. They constituted the land owing class which freely oppressed the tenant class consisting of such communities like Mappilas and Ezhavas. The law that prevailed in the land was not equalitarian. The Brahmins as a class enjoyed immunity from death penalty, while even for ordinary offences like theft the lower castes were given this inhuman punishment. They were denied even basic human rights. The backward communities (avarnas) among the Hindus were subjected to several other social handicaps. They were denied admission to temples, Schools and Public services. The evils of untouchability, unapproachability and unseeability were practiced. The Practice of pollution (theendal) was widely observed. Many of the public highways were inaccessible to the members of the lower castes including the Ezhavas. No low caste Hindu could walk along the approach roads to the temples a privilege enjoyed even by Christians and Muslims. There were innumerable sub castes among the various castes and between them there was no inter marriage or even inter-dining. This tan was strictly enforced among the Nairs and the Ezhavas. Thus the Pulayas were considered untouchable by the Ezhavas and they were denied admission into temples owned by them. The Social scene in Kerala presented many such paradoxes. The caste system operated itself in such an irrational and oppressive manner that Swami Vivekananda who visited the state in 1892 called Kerala 'The madhouse of India'.

Making the social structure more complex, there existed several obsolete customs which stood in the way of the socio-economic progress of various sections of society. The traditional Marumakkathayam system according to which inheritance was traced through the female line, there by denying to the sons any share in the property and wealth of the father, caused considerable tensions among the Nairs and Ezhavas. The observance of such social customs as Talikettukalyam, Tirandukuli and Pulikudi led to much wasteful expenditure and brought about the economic ruin of several middle class families. There were also such social evils as polygamy and child marriage.

Even the Namboodiris who were at the apex of the caste structure suffered from the operation of obsolete customs western education was taboo to them. The custom of permitting only the eldest son in the Namboodiri Illam to marry Namboodiri girls led to the majority of Namboodiri women remaining spinsters all through their life. To make matters worse was the institution of Smartha Vicharam, the caste tribunal which tried Namboodiri women accused of sexual misconduct.

It was against this background that social reform movements aimed at the modernisation of Kerala society were started since the latter half of the 19th century. The social reform movements like the Brahma samaj, Aryasamaj, Ramakrishna Mission, theosophical society etc. which originated outside the state had only marginal effect on Kerala society. Mention may be made of Swami Agamananda the founder of the Ramakrishna Advaita Ashramam at Kaladi who espoused such noble causes as eradication of caste buriers and Harijan uplift and left his indelible mark on the socio-cultural life of modern Kerala. But the reform movements which made the greatest impact on the public life of Kerala were of local origin and were led by Chattampi Swamikal (1853-1924) and Sri Narayana Guru (1856-1926).

Chattampi Swamikal

Chattampi Swamikal was a Nair reformist who revolted against the existing social order in which the Brahmins enjoyed a monopolistic position. He wanted the major Hindu communities like the Nairs and Ezhavas to play their legitimate role in Society. The work of Chattampi Swamikal was mainly confined to the ranks of the Nair community for he believed that a social awakening among them would serve as an inspiration to the non-Brahmin castes and set the pace for the great social change. He worked in close Co-operation with Sri Narayana Guru in the common cause of Hindu social and religions regeneration. He raised his voice against such evils as untouchability, Sub-caste barriers and observance of irrational social practices like Talikettukalyanam and Tirandukuli.

The Nairs eventually came to have their own social organisations to work for the social and economic uplift of the community the Malayali sabha started in 1886 and the Keralaya Nair Samajam established in 1905 were among the earliest of the Nair social organisations the general impression was that the Keralaya Nair Samajam was not doing anything tangible for the uplift and welfare of the Nairs. So a group of fourteen young men under the leadership of Mannath Padmanabhan met at Cchanganasseri on October 31, 1914 and launched a new organisation named the Nair Service Society K. Kolappan was its first president and Mannath Padmanabhan the first secretary. The N.S.S. took a definite stand in favour of the abolition of untouchability. It also took effective steps to popularise. Misra Bhojanam (inter dining). The initiative taken by the N.S.S in getting the Marumakkathayam law of inheritance amended deserves special mention. In deference to the views of the society the Travancore government passed in 1912 the first Nair Act which provided for Tavazhi partition of Nair Tarawads and sanctioned half of the self-acquired property of a male to his Children and the other half to his nephews. As this Act did not satisfy the progressive sections of the Nair community, the government passed second Nair Act in 1925 providing for individual partition and denying to the nephews all claim to the properties of their uncles. The Nair Act served as the model for similar legislation in respect of the Ezhavas and the Nanjanad Vellalas in Travancore.

Sri Narayana Guru

Sri Narayana Guru was an Ezhava saint who made a solid contribution to the social change in Kerala like Chattampi Swamikal he too revolted against Brahmin supremacy and campaigned for the mitigation of the rigors of caste. He consecrated shrines in several parts of Kerala for the worship of the Ezhavas and permitted entry into them by the pulayas and other low castes considered inferior to the Ezhavas in the social scale. The Ezhavas themselves officiated as priests in the temples founded by the Swamiji. He also campaigned against the observance of such practices as Talikettukalyanam, Tirandukuli etc among the Ezhavas and achieved a large measure of success in persuading them to give up these practices the Guru exhorted the Ezhavas and other backward castes to take to modern education and industrial and commercial pursuits for achieving their social and economic advancement. He founded in 1903 the Sree Narayana Dharma Paripalana Yogam to work for the social and spiritual uplift of the Ezhavas and other backward classes and foster self-respect among them Dr. Palpu, Kumaran Asan and N. Govindan were closely associated with the Guru during the early phase of its activities. Sree Narayana Guru had a highly eclectic outlook in religions matters and this is evidenced by his famous dictum 'One caste, one religion, one god for man'. He has been rightly hailed as the 'Father of Modern Kerala Renaissance the social revolution unleashed by him helped considerably in preparing the ground for political awakening in modern Kerala. The Swamiji attained Samadhi at Varkala in 1928 and the place has become an important centre of pilgrimage.

Several other lenders who hailed from the Ezhava community derived inspiration from the teachings of Sree Narayana Guru made their contribution to the social reform movement of the times T. K. Madhavan who edited the Desabhimani and C. V. Kunjiraman who hailed from Mayyanad also worked for the cause of Ezhava uplift C. V. Kunjiraman started a School at Mayyanad and also the newspaper Kerala Kaumudi to further the ideals of Sree Narayana.

K. Ayyappan founded the Sahodara Sangham in 1917 with the object of eradicating the evils of caste and popularising the idea of Misra-bhojanam among the Ezhavas and other low castes. In the Malabar area C. Krishnan the editor of the Mitavadi campaigned vigorously of the eradication of untouchability. In November 1917 he defied the order of Malabar collector denying freedom to the Ezhavas and other backward classes to walk along the approach roads to the Tali temple at Kozhikode. The incident symbolised the new awakening among the backward classes and focused public attention on the need for early eradication of untouchability.

Ayyankali and others

Another noted social reformer of models Kerala who deserves special mention is Ayyankali (1866-1941) the pulaya leader who got inspiration from the work of Sree Narayana Guru. He founded in 1907 the Sadhu Jana Paripalana Yogam and organised the Depressed classes in Travancore into a potent force. It was as a result of his endeavors that the pulaya community secured the right to walk in freedom along the public roads in Travancore. In recognition of his outstanding services to the Harijan community Ayyankali was nominated by the Travancore government as a member of the

Sri Mulam Praja Sabha and this provided him with a respectable field wherefrom he could carry on his fight for social equality and justice with the goodwill and Co-operation of the leaders of other communities what over progress the Harijans have achieved in recent decades in Kerala is in no small measure due to the untiring and selfless efforts of Ayyankali.

Yogakshema Sabha

In order to eradicate some social disabilities among the Namboodiri the Yogakshema Sabha was started in about 1910-11 to ensure the all-round progress of the community. The slogan of the Sabha was 'Make Namboodiri a human being' Kurur Unni Namboodiri who emerged as the leader of the progressive section fought relentlessly and stressed the need for the Namboodiris to take to English education. The Namboodiri Yuvajana Sangham with a radical plan of action was launched by the great social activites V. T. Bhattathirippad and K. N. Kuttan Namboodiri. A mugazine by name 'Unni Namboodiri' was published by them to disseminate progressive ideas among the members of the community and achieve the goal of social revolution. As a consequence of the active advocacy of social reform by the Yogakshema Sabha, in Travancore the Malayala Brahmin Regulation made arrangements for the better management of the Namboodiri Illam and did away with some of the uncertainties in the existing law of inheritance and succession.

Vakkam Abdul Khadir Maulavi

The social reform movement in Kerala was not confined to the Hindu community alone. The Muslims who were educationally backward were also affected by the winds of change. One of the most important of the Muslim social reformers was Vakkam Abdul Khadar Maulavi (1873-1932) A scholar in Arabic, Persian, Urdu and Malayalam he laboured hard for the social uplift and moral regeneration of his community. He exhorted the Muslims to discard all un-Islamic practices to take to English education in increasing numbers and to play an active part in modern progressive movements. He edited periodicals like Muslim and Deepika the Swadeshabhimani edited by K.Ramakrishna Pillai was owned by him. On the pattern of the communal organisations started by the Ezhavas and the Nairs, the Maulavi Sahib also founded such organisations like Travancore Muslim Mahajana Sabha and Chirayinkil Taluk Muslim Sangam for carrying on active work for the social uplift of the Muslims and dissemination of liberal ideas among them. The progress of the Muslim community of Kerala in the educational and social fields is largely due to the pioneering work done by Maulavi Sahib

Catholic Mahajana Sabha

The religious minorities of the Christian were also influenced by the winds of change blowing across the social scene in Kerala. In 1905 was formed the Catholic Mahajana Sabha and in 1911 the Christian Mahajana Sabha. These organisations took up with the governments in Travancore and Cochin such issues of concern to the community as child marriage, dowry and the lack of a clearly defined law of inheritance. The Christian succession Act II of 21 December 1916 was passed in Travancore to codify and amend the laws relating to intestate succession among Christians. An Act on similar line was passed in Cochin too in 1921.

Movements for the eradication of untouchability

The most important of the social reform movements of Kerala was the agitation for the removal of untouchability. One of the earliest leaders of the movement was C. Krishnan, editor of Mithavadi. Another able advocate in Kerala was T. K. Madhavan, who championed the cause of untouchables in the columns of

Desabhimani which he edited. The first major struggle was the famous Vaikkom Satyagraha (1924-25)

Vaikkom Satyagraha

T. K. Madhavan, K. P. Kesavamenan, Mannath Padmanabhan, Changanassery Parameswaran Pillai, C. V. Kunchiraman and K. Kolappan were associated with the Vaikkom satyagraha. One of the highlights of the Satyagraha was the Savarna Jatha organised under the leadership of Mannath Padmanabhan by the caste Hindus who supported the movement. The members of the Yatha came to Trivandrum and submitted their demand before the Regent Setu Lekshmi Bai. The vaikkom Satyagraha and the Savarna yatha helped to influence public opinion in the state in favour of temple entry through the Satyagrahas at vaikkom were arrested and harassed in many ways during the 20 month old struggle, the Satyagraha finally ended in success in 1925 due to the intervention of Mahatma Gandhi. The approach roads to the temple were formally opened to all Hindus, irrespective of caste. But this concession was not extended to the Avarnas in the case of other temples in Travancore. Hence movements for getting the approach roads opened to the Avarnas were organised in such centers as Ambalapuzha, Tiruvarpu, Suchindram etc during the period following the successful termination of the vaikkom Satyagraha.

Guruvayur Satyagraha

One of the most important struggles connected with the campaign for the eradication of untouchability was the Guruvayur Satyagraha (1931-32) The Satyagraha was started on November 1, 1931 under the auspices of the Kerala provincial congress in order to get the Guruvayur temple opened to all Hindus. The leader of the Satyagraha was K. Kolapan and the captain of the volunteers corps A.K.Gopalan. The Satyagraha attracted countrywide attention and political workers from all over India converged on Gruruvayur to extend help to the Satyagrahas. The zamorin, who was the trustee of the temple adopted an uncompromising attitude towards the demand of temple entry. One of the incidents connected with the Satyagraha was the assault on A. K. Gopalan on December 26 by the opponents of the Satyagraha movement. It roused the passions of the people and they attempted to force entry into the temple by removing the barricades. The temple was closed and all pujas suspended for about a month. The Satyagraha had run its course for 10 months when K. Kolappan entered on an indefinite fast before the temple on September 21, 1932, but he have up the fast on October 2, 1932 on Gandhiji's advice. A limited referendum was held thereafter under the auspices of the congress among the Hindus of Ponnani Taluk in order to ascertain the views of the people on the issue of temple entry. About 70% of the people signified their approval of temple entry for Harijans thus, though the Guruvayur Satyagraha failed to achieve its immediate objective, it had helped to create a climate in favour of the eradication of untouchability.

Temple Entry

The movement for temple entry registered its crowning victory when Sri Chithira Tirunal Balaramavarma, the Maliaraja of Travancore issued his famous Temple Entry proclamation on November 12, 1936. The proclamation which is the first of its kind is a historic document Gandhiji hailed it as a 'Miracle of modern times' and a smriti which is the people's charter of spiritual emancipation.

The temple Entry proclamation of Maharaja of Travancore came as a bomb-Shell in orthodox Hindu circles, but it gave a message of hope and good cheer to the down-trodden Harijan and other backward classes. It brought about a silent and bloodless revolution in Hindu society. However, it took one more decade for the reform to be introduced in Cochin and Malabar. The Temple Entry Authorisation proclamation V of 1123 (1947-48) issued by the Maharaja of Cochin opened the temples in that state to all Hindus, irrespective of caste. The Madras Temple Entry Act of 1947 extended this reform to the Malabar area with the dawn of Independence, untouchability has been abolished by legislation and those who practice it have been made liable to punishment. The historic movement for the eradication of untouchability in Kerala was thus crowned with success.

Conclusion

The efforts of Sri Narayana Guru, Chattampi Swamikal and the communal organisations like NSS and SNDP paved the way for a hew social order in Kerala. The unlawful customs prevailed in the country were vanished away and the people irrespective of caste and colour developed a modern and progressive social outlook. The impact of education and the increasing Socio-economic awareness served as a major factor in political consciousness among the people. This intimately served the larger cause of the struggle for freedom and responsible government in Kerala. Thus the social renaissance of the 19th and 20the centuries can be considered as an important episode in the history of Kerala and also for the freedom struggle of India.

Selected Bibliography

Bhaskaran Unni.P., *Pathonpatham Noottandile Keralam*, Thrissur, 1988

SreedharaMenon, A, *Kerala and Freedom struggle*, D.C.Books, Kottayam, 1997.

Sreedhara Menon, *A, A survey of Kerala Histom*, Viswanathan Printers and Publices, Madras.

Sreedhara Menon, A, *Trivandrum District Gazetteer*, Trivandrum, 1962.

SreedharaMenon, *A, Kerala History and its Makers*, 2008.

Suresh Kumar, *Political Education in Kerala*, 1859-1938.Delhi

Velayudhan P.S., *SNDP Yogacharithram*, Quilon, 1978.

Mathrubhumi Daily, 14 February 2011, Trivandrum

Namboodirippad EMS, *Kerala Society and Politics: A historical Survey*, Newdelhi, 1984

Ramachandran K, *History of Trade union movement in Kerala*, Trivandrum, 2006.

7

The Unsung Freedom Fighter Mr. K. Perumal Panicker from Kottar

Dr. G. Subbiah

Perumal Panicker was born in Kottar, a business centre in 1878. His father was Kunjananjan Panicker. He had four sisters and two brothers. In the mid of Nagerkovil town, he had a toll gate. He was engaged in salt business. His business shop was called as 'UppuPirai'. When rice was sold for 25 paisa, Rs.1 lakh in his hand was an ordinary event. Besides business, he had a great thirst to get freedom for his motherland. He was basically a serious congress man. He wore dress as the same of Mahatma Gandhi. He was attracted by the Gandhian ideology. Perumal Panicker participated in the freedom struggles. He was a notable leader in the suchindram temple entry movement. He actively took part in the movement with Dr. M.E. Naidu and Mr. Pillai.

Under the leadership of Naidu, firing of foreign cloth campaign took place in Vadiveeswaram sanskrit school campus in 1921. Syehu Thambi Pavalar gave a revolutionary talk for an hour. The other important leaders who took part in that campaign were Perumal Panicker, Hyder Sahib, Theroor Subramaniya Pillai, Vadiveeswarm Palaniyandi Iyer, Nataraja Iyer and Sathya Vakeeswara Iyer.

In a letter to the Dewan of Travancore by Naidu (secretary, Suchindrumsathagraha committee) wrote as I have the honour to submit that the Suchindramsatygraha committee met on 6th June of 1926 and passed some resolutions.

A meeting of Persons from Nanjilnadu who are interested in the proposed Suchindram satyagraha conducted at Naidu's residence at kottar on Tuesday at 6 P.M. to concert measures for conducting satyagraha at Suchindram for gaining admission to the members of depressed class into the streets of Suchindram. By unanimous consent Subramoneya Pillai of Theroor was elected as President.

The following resolutions were passed. That meeting resolved that with to get admission to the members of the depressed classes in the Suchindram streets. Regular satyagraha should be organised. The general organisation and the conduct of satyagraha shall vest in a committee called the Suchindram satyagraha working committee. It composed of the following members with power to add Naidu, Perumal Panicker, P.C. Thanu Malaya Perumal and Gandhidas, Muthuswamy were elected as secretary, treasurer, publicity officer and captain respectively. The other members were M.Sivathanoo Pillai from Nagercoil, Chidambarathanu Pillai from Nagercoil, N. Agastialingom Pillai from Aramboly, P. Swaminatha Pillai from Nagercoil, P. Subramania Iyer from Nagercoil, M. Sudalamuthu Pillai from kottar, M. Mathevan Pillai from Parakkai, T. Muthu Karuppa Pillai from kottar, P.C. Thanoomalaya Pillai from kottar and C.Gandhi Das and C. Muthuswamy from Theroor. It was resolved that M. Sivathanoo Pillai and four office bearers had to formed the executive committee. It was also resolved that the treasurer should immediately open a satyagraha fund. It was also resolved that the executive committee should make the necessary arrangements and start satyagraha on Wednesday the 14th of Thy 1926. The executive committee conducted on 7th July of 1926. It was resolved to commence satyagraha at 8 A.M on Wednesday 14th Thy 1926.

T. Kumaran thampi, inspector of police, Edalakudy gave a report to the commissioner of police on 30th January of 1926, the report was as follows: I beg to submit that day also satyagraha work was begun at the eastern road in sannadi street at Suchindram at 8 A.M. Ramaswami Naicker of Erode was present this morning. Naidu and Periyar had a look at Suchindram and gone away. There were ten volunteers and Captain Muthuswami. They had gone away. They were prevented from going forward by the anti – satyagraha at Suchindram. Afternoon they were removed and other party of volunteers posted there. Further two volunteers tried at the lane connecting sannadhi street and main road they were also prevented by anti-satyagrahis. That day satyagraha work was closed at 5 P.M. Then there went an open meeting of the satyagrahis on the river side in which Sivathanu Pillai from Nagercoil, Naidu, Ramasami Naicker of Erode, Perumal Panicker of kottar delivered lectures on temple entry work and satyagraha campaign at Travancore. The meeting was commenced at 6 P.M. and closed at 8 P.M. The satyagrahis expressed that tomorrow was being Sunday there would not be regular satyagraha work, but there would be a satyagraha marching by the volunteers with bhajan at 8 A.M. and returning to their asramam at 10 P.M. A police constable was present at the spot throughout and the situation was reported to be silence.

Inspector of Police, Edalakudy submitted report to the commissioner of police, Travancore, Trivandrum on 27th February of 1926. He reported that, I beg to submit that that day also satyagraha movement began as usual on the northern road and sannadhi street in Suchindram.

The volunteers were present at 6 A.M. and their opponents also were there on the spot. At 10.30 A.M. a party of satyagraha volunteers, 24 in number with their secretary, Naidu and treasurer Perumal Panicker of kottar and others visited the two places of satyagraha in Suchindram and told that they were not prepared to go to the streets in Suchindram until the obstructionists excise pity on them and call them voluntarily and the present them voluntarily and that the present satyagraha movement had therefore been stopped temporarily from that time. So the volunteers who present there were withdrawn and they all went away to kottar.

Regarding Vaikom satyagraha, sincere thanks was put forward by the life partners of great business people of kottar to Maharani sethulekshmi bai. Mrs. K. Perumal Panicker, Mrs. R. Ramalingam, Mrs. K. Ponniya, Mrs. P. Thiraviam Panicker, Mrs. S. Shanmugam Panicker and Mrs. A. Saravanai Panicker, Kottar stated as we ezhava women's of kottar offer sincere thanks for your highness's sympathy towards untouchables and warmly pray for your higness' long life and Prosperity.

On 8th October of 1927, Mahatma Gandhi along with his wife Kasthuri Bai came through Tirunelveli came to Nagercoil. A great welcome was given to Gandhiji. Gandhiji stayed at Perumal Panicker's house.

Perumal Panicker's House

When he was staying there, perumal panicker's daughter Swarnama was also stayed with him and she had a lot of jewels on her neck. Gandhiji watched the same and asked her "whether these jewels are going to give her education or good qualities in her life; you are living and will be living with fear regarding the safety of these jewels." Gandhiji then asked if she would give those jewels for the welfare of our nation.

Gandhi asked in Guajarati language and Raja Gopala Chari translated it into Tamil. She saw her father. Perumal Panicker reacted positively. She then immediately gave those jewels to Gandhiji.

At the public meeting, thereceived jewels were auctioned and the money was handed over to Gandhiji for our freedom struggle.

Only because of Gandhiji's stay at Perumal Panicker's house, the street was named as Gandhi Street. Sree Narayana Guru Marriage hall of Ezhava Trust is located in this street.

Thus the contribution of Perumal Panicker for the upliftment of the downtrodden people, temple entry and our freedom movement are remarkable one.

References

Sivathanu Pillai.M., Parattapadatha Poratta Veerar

Dinathanthi15.08.2004.

Issac Jeyadhass.S., Kanniyakumari Maavattavum India Suthandra Poratta Iyakkavum, Mecalroy Publications, Villukkuri,2014, p.

Krishna Moni: Dr. M. E. "Naidu as a Nationalist Research," *Journal of Indian studies at rjisacjournal*.com accessed on 21st July of 2022.

Lakshmi Raghnandham (2010) *The life and times of Maharani SethuLekshmi Bayi, The last queen of Travancore, Maharani Sethu Lakshmi Bayi Memorial charity trust*, Bangalore.

Indian Muslim Legends: Sathavathani Shikh Thambi Pavalar at Pavalar blog.com accessd on 22nd July of 2022.

Nanchilnad Ramachandran P (1979), M.E. Naidu and Suchindram Satyagraha, *Sivakami Panting house*, kottar, Nagercoil PP. 24 – 26, 30-31, 38.

Personal Interviews

Sree Ram, Gandhi Street, Kottar, 31.03.2022, 03.04.2022

Sidhartha Hamsapathy, Gandhi Street, Kottar, 04.04.2022.

1. C.Aruljothi, S.Ramasamy, *Pilgrimage Tourism Socio-Economic Analysis*, MJP Publishers, Chennai, 2015, P.7
2. A.K Bhatia, *Tourism development Principles and practices*, Sterling Publishers Pvt. Ltd, New Delhi, 2009, P.307
3. VSV, *Arintha Alayankal Apurva Thagavalkal (Tamil)*, VikatanPirasuram, Chennai, 2008, P.14.
4. N.Pandurangan, *Ariyappadatha Madurai (Tamil)*, New Century Book House Pvt.Ltd., Chennai, 2018, P.10
5. *Thiruppanimalai V.22 says that the Amman Sannidhi*, Mahamandapam, first prakaram and palliarai were built by ThirumalirunjolaiMavali (1452 AD)
6. N. S.Ramaswami, *Temples of South India*, Maps and Agencies Publications, Madras, 1984, p.145.
7. B.N.Luniya, *Evolution of Indian Culture*, Educational Publishers, Agra, 1951, P.271.
8. Percy Brown, *Indian Architecture*, Taraporevala Sons Co. Private Ltd, Bombay, 1953, P.107
9. Opcite, N.Pandurangan, P.4
10. K.Palaniappan, Koil Managar (Tamil), K. Thiagarajan, (Trans), *The Great Temple of Madurai*, Arulmigu Meenakshi Sundareswarar Thirukkoil, Madurai, 2012, p.97
11. P. Rajendran & C.Santhalingam, Mamadurai (Tamil), *Pandiya Nadu Historical Research Centre*, Madurai, 2015, P.120
12. Madura A Tourist Guide Illustrated, *Asian Educational Services*, Madras, 1991, P. 122
13. Sanjay Singh, *Madurai The Madhurapuri,* Sunjoy Publisher, Agra, 2018, P.251
14. Rajesh Singh, *Pilgrimage Tourism*, Sonali Publications New Delhi, 2017, P.190
15. Ibid. P.192
16. Ibid.P.194
17. K. R. Srinivasan, *Temples of South India*, New Delhi, 1985, p. 123
18. K. V. Soundara Rajan, "Early Pandya, Muttarayar and Irukkuel Architecture",
19. Architecture ed. Pramod Chandra, New Delhi. 1975, p. 257.
20. G. Subiah, *Early Pantiyan Architecture*, Unpublished Ph.D. Thesis, Calcutta University, Calcutta, 1977, p. 252.
21. Michael W. Meister (ed.), *Encyclopaedia of Indian Temple Architecture: South India: Lower Dravidadesa*, Delhi, 1983, pp. 122-23.
22. S.I.I. Vol. XIV. no. 13
23. S.I.I. Vol. XIV. no. 36
24. K.V Soundara Raajan, *Indian Temple styles*, New Delhi197 P.119
25. Sthala varalaru The Tirumulanatha Temple at Ambasamudiram, and Devisvaramudaiyar, Appan and the Bhaktavatsala Temple at cheranmahadevi

26. A.R.E. 1916, No.640,
27. SII.VoL.XIV, No.190, pp.104-105.
28. Pandian. T.B., *The Ancient Heroes of south Indian*, Peninsula, madras, 1893., p 152.
29. A.R.E. 1916, No.629.
30. Vithuvaan Perumal, K.V., *Porunai Valam*, Chennai, 1977, p.77.
31. Arulmigu Vaithiyanatha Swamy Kovil Thala Varalaru, 1999.4-6
32. ARE., 1916, No.640SII., Vol.XIV, NO.190, pp.104-105.
33. ARE., 1916,No.626.
34. ARE, 1916, No.618-B.
35. Arulmigu Ramaswamy Thirukkovil Varalaru, 199, pp.4-6
36. E.I Vol. No.6, pp. 46-47.
37. ARE 1895, No0183.
38. Arulmigu Ammainathaswamy Thirukovil Thala varalaru, kovil
39. Veliyeedu, Cheranmahadevi, 1999, pp.3-7.
40. *Arulmigu Ramasamy Thirukovil Thala varalaru,* kovil Veliyeedu, Cheranmahadevi, 1999, pp.3-4
41. G. Subiah, *Early Pantiyan Architecture*, Unpublished Ph.D. Thesis, Calcutta University, Calcutta, 1977m p. 252.
42. Parameswaram pillai.V.R, *Temple culture of south India*, Trivandrum, 1985, p 85.

8

Impact of World Wars in Travancore's Socio-Political Environment

Dr. V. Karthik Nisha

Introduction

There were more than 800 Princely States in the sub-continent when the British people came to India for the first time and established their empire here. The socio-political environment remained more or less the same for a long time in the country in spite of certain outbursts now and than. It is with the formation of the Indian National Congress in 1885, that a live and organised movement started functioning towards effecting liberation from the foreigners and establish home rule. Just as its activities created ripples in every Princely State over the Country, Travancore also experienced a great momentum coupled with the vibrations of reforms introduced by the indigenous rulers.

During the First World War, Travancore was ruled by king Sreemoolam Thirunal. He rose to the throne in1884 and ruled the country till 1924. Nine Diwans served under him successively. Just as his predecessors, he too had acquired western education. During his long reign of forty years, history witnessed certain education landmarks such as the submission of Malayali Memorial in 1891, Chalai Mutiny of 1908, the confiscation of Swadesabhimani Press and banishing of Ramakrishna Pillai, the Students Strike of 1921 and Vaikkam Satyagraha of 1924. In between was the World War and the momentum it created in every field of human life in the Princely State of Travancore.

Cataclysms

Sreemoolam Thirunal was much influenced by Saravana, an illiterate Brahmin who was the head of the servants of the court and whose title was Foujdaar and Sankaran Thampi, the Chief Official in the court affairs.

M. Krishnan Nair was the Diwan of Travancore when the First World War broke out in 1914. He was comparatively a harmless, weakling who stood by the king in his reformary measures unlike most of his predecessors. It was in1911 that the Normal school in Trivandrum was raised to the level of a Training college and Model School was established. The Ayurveda School which later became a College also was patronised during the reign of Sreemoolam Thirunal. These institutions along with the Sanskrit school within the fort, the Medical school, the law College and SMV school, all situated in Trivandrum responded to the World War. By that time, education had given the young generation new insights into ideas like freedom, self-rule, and party politics. The teachers and senior students in these institutions were inspired by the nationalistic feelings that parvaded the whole country. They quit School and colleges and joined hands with the activists of the movements who supported, the Britishers in the war.

The Congress leaders divided among themselves in the matter of giving support to the British. However, the King and his ministry who by that time had become an alley of the British had no other option. So they stretched all possible helps to the British army that participated in the war.

Economic Crisis

The war left lasting effects in the economics and socio-political fields of India. To fulfil the growing needs of the army during the war, excess taxes were imposed on the consumer goods. This called for a hike in the price of the goods. The Diwan undertook some measures to tackle the situation, but failed miserably. The people who supported the Britishers initially now turned against them. Restlessness and chaos prevailed everywhere. The indigenous administrative system headed by Sreemoolam Thirunal proved quite inadequate to face the situation. However, since the people were mostly loyal to the king, they did not rise in a mutiny. Instead, they informed the king of their miserable conditions. The king in his turn, ordered to arrange distribution of essential goods among the people at bearable prices. This measure had however not much impact on the economic situation that existed there.

The main occupation of youngsters of the period was service in the army. Deficiency and high demand for food and scarcity of essential goods caused restlessness among them. As against their will, they were forced to serve the Britishers as well. Meanwhile, they did not have equal pay or consideration as the English soldiers enjoyed. This worsened the situation. However, both the King and the Diwan were incapable of handling the matter in a tactful manner. Hence the troubled state of mind of the soldiers affected the peace of the whole society.

During the First World War, an epidemic of influenza affected the whole of India whose mortal blow caused the death of more than one crore people. In Travancore also a large number of army men and civilians died on account of disease coupled with starvation and poverty.

An Unfulfilled Promise

When the war came to an end, the British commanders met at the Delhi Head Quarters. They recorded their sincere thanks to the King of the Princely states for having extended their support to England in the War. They made reference to Travancore also in "availing them the help of the Nair Pattalam (Soldiers) in winning the war". In gratitude, They sent to Travancore ship full of merchandise and impressed the royal members.

The Readers of the Indian National Congress supported the British ruler in the war, for they believed word of the Viceroy that they would give freedom to the country once the war ended in their favour. But no measures to effect granting self-rule to India was taken up by the British administrative head. Hence the party leaders started a strong protest movement, that left the whole of India agitated.

Social Movements

People who have acquired education started dreaming of a free country, though the concept of a united India was not yet evolved. The American-French revolutions had influenced the educated youth of the time. In Travancore, the extreme end of India, also out bursts of thought and ideals started getting moulded.

Social reformers like Ani Bessent and Dayananda Saraswathi had great influence in the society of Travancore. When the Home Rule Movement started, it had its centers in Travancore also. The war and its miseries intensified the craving of the people for freedom and self-development. Meanwhile branches of Theosophical Society also started functioning here. These organisations were a source of consolation for the grieving people of the post war society.

Dr. Hudson Speaks

Dr. Hudson who was Addl. Poltical Secretary to the Viceroy and a historian himself, has recorded his interactions with the royal family of Travancore from 1910 to 1923. "Sreemoolam Thirunal, the Maharaja of the princely state has been friendly to the office of the Viceroy, though his bureaucracy refused to oblige to him in his dealings with the British empire. Neither did he seek their full-hearted support in implementing the reforms suggested by us on the grounds that they would spoil their culture and tradition".

Dr. Hudson gives a detailed account of the pattern of society and political set up existed at that time. The war has had some impact on the economy of the state and caused some upheavals in the socio-political fields. "The deficiency of essential goods during the world war caused mush disruption in the society. People. However, educated youngsters seemed to understand the facts. British government is grateful to the princely governments to have extended their help in time of the war."

"People started consuming non-vegetarian food. The Press criticized both the indigenous kings and the British rule for the miseries of the people. Office of the Viceroy directly issued orders to provide food and grains to the poor people in the state."

Dr.Hudson quotes certain newspapers where the socio-political and religious reformers gave vent to their protests against Indians supporting the British government in the war. Measures to tackle the situation were also undertaken though insufficiently. Sacks of rice, vegetables, salt, spices etc were transported to Travancore from neighbouring territories. But since the sales tax had also an equal hike, the King failed to satisfy the people. This gave rise to a middle class who hated the royal rule of the state. They joined Indian National Congress and Other Small political groups whom the police shadowed and tried to crush frequently.

The use of intoxicants, though secretly, became widespread. People tried to do away their frustrations using intoxicants. Luxury life of people had its end. Here and there the Nair-Soldiers refused to obey their superior officers and showed signs of mutiny. However, wide outbursts did not occur.

Various Responses

Great writes and Masterminds who lived During the period under the patronage of the royal family such as A.R.Rajaraja Varma, Ulloor.S.Parameswarayyar, Kumaranasan, Prof.V.Krishnan Thambi, C.V.Raman Pillai, C.V.Kunhiraman, Kesari Balakrishna Pillai, E.V.Krishna pillai and others responded to the social, political and economic change caused by the war in the society. They spoke at the meeting, discussed and criticized the stances of the rulers at the developments. Among these culture leaders, Kesari Bala Krishna Pillai was the fiercest in crticising the reigning royal family. His journal "Swadesabhimani" reported the unhealthy pratices prevailed in the administration and among the bureaucracy. He tried to bring to the notice of the people and the authorities how corruption at various levels caused deterioration of the society.

Conclusion

A close study of the history of Travancore during the First World War shows how the battle would affect the socio-cultural life of the people and the political and economic structure of the society. It is found that the vibrations of the vibrations of the war as a whole intensified the nationalistic spirits in the people and augmented the process of obtaining freedom for the country. A crisis often unities the people of various standards and interests ultimately. Here also the people of Travancore became more aware of the need for self-rule, once they were exposed to the miseries of the war.

Reference Books

Dr. K.K.N. Kurup, *1982 – Modern History,* Kerala Bhasha Institute, Trivandrum P.Shangoonny Menon, 1973 – History of Travancore Kerala Bhasha Institute, Trivandrum

Dr. Naduvattam Gopalakrishnan, 1990 – Kerala Charitha Dharakal National Book stall, Kottayam K.P.Padmanabha menon, 1989 – Travancore Dynasty Kerala Sahithya Academy, Thrissur Dr.V.S.Sharma, 1992 – Thiruvithamcore Rajavamsam Dr.V.S.Sharma, Tvm

Keasri Balakrishna Pillai, 1984 – Charithrathinte Adiverukal Kerala Sahithya Academy P.A.Warrier, 1988 – History of Independence Kairali Children's Book Trust, Kottayam

K. Damodaran & C.Narayana Pillai, 1957 – Kerala Swathanthriya Samaram Public Relations Department of Kerala, Trivandrum.

K. Sivasankaran Nair, 2004 – Ananthapuri Noottandukaliloode Current Books, Kottayam K.Kunjippakky, 1984 – World History Language Institute, Trivandrum.

9

Human Figurines of the Indus Civilisation

Dr. D. Vinoba Gladis

Introduction

Besides pottery, numerous human figurines of terracotta were found at the Indus valley sites: usually female, a few male figurines and animals, and a few stones statuettes of sandstone and limestone, the latter from Harappa only. There were also some model animals made of copper and bronze, and a couple of human figurines in bronze. A few objects were made in shell and faience.

All these have been discussed in detail by Mohenjodaro and the Indus Civilisation and then in Further Excavations at Mohenjodaro as also by Vats in Excavations at Harappa only. Those discovered later at Chanhudaro were discussed by Mackay. Now it is indeed surprising that so many females' figurines should be found at Harappa and Mohenjodaro, and almost none at Lothal, Kalibangan and Surkotada, or at Amri, Kot Diji and now Gumla in Pakistan. However, the Indian as well as the Pakistani sites have yielded a few specimens of model animals in terracotta, and one or two in copper-bronze.

In the first place the model animals in terracotta were all made for children as toys, or some were toys for children and some made for other purposes. When archaeology has acquired a new dimension granted that some precocious child or children would make such toys, and their parents bake them in fire, would these be made by children in several families, as would appear by the distribution of these animals at Harappa and Mohenjodaro.

What is most probable is that there were types of model animal, good, bad, indifferent, made either for different purpose or different classes of people, distinguished by wealth and social status.

Unfortunately, Marshall, Mackay and Vats have recorded all the finds together, although mentioning their location. However, a study of all these finds should be made, nothing not only but the general location, that is the depth at which the model animals or figurine was found, but the room or the house, its general situation and other objects found with it.

Two Stones Statuettes from Harappa

It is indeed unfortunate that since these statuettes were found some 50 years ago, no efforts was made either to search for more of such specimens or to clear away the mist of uncertainty about their exact stratigraphical position. The red sandstone statuette is a torso, headless and broken just above both the knee. It was found by Vats in the third stratum in a part of the site at Harappa where no objects whatever of the historic age have appeared. This stone is not available in Punjab, but can had in the Vindhyan range between Kota and Bharatpur or Mathura. "The treatment of torso" as Marshall admirably described the statuette," could hardly be simpler or more direct. The pose is a frontal one with shoulders well back and abdomen slightly prominent; but the beauty lies in the refined and wonderfully truthful modeling of the fleshy parts.

An interesting feature in this statuette, as in the other, is the technique adopted for fixing the head and the arms, and the nipples of the breasts. Socket-holes have been provided in the neck and the shoulders for attaching these as well as the nipples. As Marshall has noted this technique is without a parallel in the historic as well as proto historic cultures in India. It has not been found in any sculpture at Mohenjodaro or any other Harappan site. However, as well be pointed below, this was a special technique developed by the Indus artist for making small figures with moveable limbs such as the head, arms and legs. This technique is seen in several toys of terracotta as well as faience.

Further in the red stone statuette there is a large circular depression in front of each shoulder, with a smaller circular protuberance broken off in the middle of it. It is not yet clears what these depressions were for. Possibly these were intended, as pointed out by Marshell, to be inlaid with circular ornaments, and in this connection draws our attention to circlets in the same position on a terracotta figurine from Baluchistan.

The dark grey stone statuette is of a different nature than the one previously discussed. The dark grey stone might be available further north around Taxila, but not in the river in Punjab. "It is the figure of a danger, standing on his right leg, with the body from the waist upward bent well round to the left, both arms thrown out in the same direction, and the left leg raised high in front". Marshall thought that the contours of the body appeared soft and effeminate. Still the figure was that of a male, and it seems that it was "ithphallic." Marshall conjectured that the figure might represent Nataraja, but such a view would be an anachronism, though such and the probable pose of the leg. Whatever it may have been, as Marshall further said, no parallel to this statuette is to be found among Indian sculptures of the later period.

Sir Mortimer Wheeler also recognised the artistic greatness of these statuettes. Though he doubled their attribution to the Indus Civilisation, he regarded them as masterpieces of "miniature modeling" Allchin thought the doubt was misplaced, for, as pointed out by Marshall, the technique employed has so far, remained unique.

In this all important matter, Greek artistry could possibly have been anticipated by sculptors of a far-off age, on the banks of the Indus, Marshall drew the right conclusion that we also had drawn independently, namely that the Indus engraver copula and did anticipate the Greek in the delineation of animal forms.

Dancer in bronze

This small figure was found at Mohenjodaro. It is too small, a figurine of 4.25 ins. height, said to be rather rough workmanship with disproportionately long arms and legs. Hence Marshall thought it was a caricature. Like a good caricature, it gave a vivid impression of the young aboriginal nautch girl, her hand on her hip in half-impudent posture, and the legs slightly forward, as she beats time to the music with her feet. The modeling of the black, hips and buttocks, even in a small figure as this, is quite effective. Hence Marshall judged this as an instance of sound observation on the part of the artist. "The abandon expressed in face and links is quite realistic."

Sir Mortimer Wheeler, while endorsing this opinion, even went further in his appreciation. He said, "this bronze dancing girl is the most remarkable of the Indus figurines. Pert and pertinent, she is naked except for her necklace and her head, expressively tilted, is a skilful impression of an aboriginal type."

That this did not constitute solitary evidence of casting well-modeled figurines in the round was proved when Mackay found another such figure, also from Mohenjodaro.

It is of bronze, 5.2 ins. in height. Exceptionally well modeled figure of a dancing girl, it has suffered from corrosion, and the finer details have been lost. The name artist might have made both the figures, with probably the same dancer in view, but standing in different postures. This absolutely frontal position is usually one with a dancer adopts at the conclusion of a dancer. In both figures one hand is on the hip, and the other brought in front of the body with the hand curved slightly upwards as if it is to hold something. In both figures the limbs, particularly the arms and the legs, as in the much later Warangal figures from Andhra Pradesh, are disproportionately elongated. Otherwise she stands erect with her feet close together, and if her feature were well preserved, she would wear the same disdainful expression. A more detailed study of these poses might help to identify the poses with their traditional names.

Semi-artistic Figures and Figurines

Most of these figurines are found in Harappa and Mohenjodaro, and some at Chanhudaro, hardly 6ins. in height usually about 4 ins. A few have been found at other sites such as Amri, Kot Diji, Gumla, in Pakistan, and Lothal, Kalibangan and Surkotada in India. While the non-occurrence at some sites might be attributed to the restricted area of excavation, this cannot be said of Lothal and Kalibangan. At these sites animal figurines both in terracotta and metal have been found, but not human figurines.

So in the account which follows, the human figurines from Mohenjodaro, Harrappa and Chanhudaro, have been discussed in that order, as it facilitates reference. It would appear from a re-reading of the accounts of Marshall, Mackay, Vats as well as brief comments by Wheeler and Allchin, that only a few striking figurines such as female figurines with fan-shaped, pannier head-dress, or the male figurines with half-closed eyes, beard or shaven upper lip, have received the attention they deserve. Many others, thought described in detail by Mackay, and a few also referred to by Vats, have remained unknown to scholar, students and the general reader.

It was a revelation for me to realise that the Harappans were after all not so much materialistic or religious or cult-minded that they ignored other aspects of daily life. The appearance of men, women and children, or the antics of animals like the squirrel did appeal to them. In actual facts these are the only miniature or otherwise models in terracotta, faience, and metal in the whole range of Indian art which do record the ordinary activities of life, historic or prehistoric.

The few terracottas from Kausambi, Ahichhatra and other sites in U.P., those from Taxila, or from Andhra, Satavahana sites like Ter and Kondapur, are primarily of a cult type. They may give us some idea of the current hair styles, but they do not portray many others facets of life.

In a few extant examples that artist has tried to portray the beauty of hair in both men and women, in others the fingers of the hands and feet. He has been attracted by the rotundity of a not-too-tall, pregnant women. This might be a caricature as Wheeler says, but we do not find caricatures again until the modern age. Lastly there are a few terracotta's, masks as well as solid figurines, where one notices attempts at portraying facial expression.

Realism in the Women's Torso

In the numerous figurines found at Harappa, Mohenjodaro, and Chanhudaro, the female breast are mostly shown in the crudest possible manner. A first impression on looking at these figures would be that either the artist did not know how to portray the female would be that either the artist did not know how to portray the female bust, or that these were only impressionistic figures, probably for cult purposes or toys. However in a few cases even these terracotta figurines exhibit well-modeled busts. When this feature is found associated with a very slim waist one has to conclude that this was the ideal of female beauty, even in Harappan times. This survived and appears in the early historical period, in the Yaksinis from Mathura. One has just to place side by side the figure from the lower levels at Mohenjodaro and the Mathura bracket figures. While the waist is highly attenuated in the former, the breasts are surprisingly well modeled and not exaggerated, and so also are the thighs.

That this part of women's anatomy was regarded as a sign of beauty and that its exposure was deliberately attempted is nowhere better illustrated than in another figure. Unlike numerous terracotta figures, here the back and front of the women's body are covered from the knee up to the breast. The latter is fully exposed, as in cretan figures. Her beauty is enhanced by an unusually large number of necklace, which hides the rest of the chest, and the entire neck up to the chin. In this figure alone the navel is concealed, otherwise it is as always shown as I the figures of the historic period.

There are a few model figurines which are described as portraying women kneading dough in a shallow rectangular trough. Apparently this description is wrongly, for such a pose is not convenient, (as far as known to me and never adopted for kneading doughty. This pose is most suitable for winnowing the calf, etc. from grain, which is also indicated by the shape of the tray that is straight – sided. This in fact is a winnowing basket or tray. In another example a women is shown carrying loaves in a platter, or in a basket kept over her head. It is interesting to see how the artist has tried to convey this idea. Evidently, either because this is a miniature terracotta model, or because the artist has no sense of perspective, or because he wants to show what the contents of the basket are, he shows the basket resting at an angle on the hand.

Headwear and Hairdressing

In the art of the early historic period or later, queens and goddesses are rarely shown with head-dress such as a mukuta (crown), even though they might be accompanying their consorts. This is not the case in Indus terracottas. Here besides the commonly illustrated, fan shaped, or pannier-like head-dresses, one can count at least four or five other fashions for adoring the head of women.

The Indus artist, whenever he chose, carefully depicted the method of dressing the hair. On seeing the illustration or the person, one could say whether a comb with fine teeth or large teeth was used, and the nature of the style adopted. Besides the well-known heads of steatite or limestone, showing the careful, even mechanical, way of grooming the hair and beard, there are two tiny ones illustrated by Mackay. The first is a fragment in black steatite of a women, now only 1.1 ins. in height. Only the black of the head remains, but it was realistically carved to represent flowing hair, well-oiled and groomed.

Portrait of Yogi

The bust is exceptionally smooth with almost a polished surface, a contemplative look, and above all a shawl with its trefoil decoration, the orb of which matches with that of circular (ornament) on forehead and on the armlet. This symmetrical composition is intentional and must be significant. As Mackay thought, here there is a definite attempt at portraiture, possibly of a curly figure or a personage who was deified. Though the chamber in which it was found, was "of most peculiar constitution," sill it could be regarded as a temple.

Marshall, who had a much better knowledge of Indian culture, thought that this yogi-like, thick-lipped person, with the broad nose, low forehead, and stretched neck did not represent any particular individual; but that it was a conventional representation of a deity or religious teacher.

The facial features again are interesting. The mouth is small with fleshy lip, and the chin prominent. A curious projection just below the chin may be a crude attempt at a beard, or it may be the Adam's apple. The eyes are mere slits, and were formerly inlaid with some plastic material. The nose is small, and so is the cranium, this being in contrast to the broad, grey face. The features are quite expensive. The check bones are very prominent, wide apart, and of medium height, with deep-set orbits. The eyes are almond-shaped and slightly wider than those in other figures with a provision for an inlay.

Masks

Horned terracotta masks have been found at Mohenjodaro, but surprisingly not at all Harappa, which had yielded so many human figurines not at all at Harappa, which has only remarked on the likely levels at Mohenjodaro "have very oblique Mongolian eye which were carefully touched up" shows that these masks, whatever their function, have an artistic value. They portray truthfully whatever they were intended to portray. They might be decorative and /or religious, but they also tell us that the people of Mohenjodaro had a clear idea of what a Mongolian looked like, from the north-eastern frontier.

Four masks from the early levels were found between the height of 13.4 ft. and 22.3ft. at very many places. The first one appeals to me much more by its fine, peaceful expression, and it is even more beautiful than No. 25-26 from the Upper level, which is discussed below. It reminds me of similar expressions on the Buddha, Bodhisattvas, and Brahmanical god such as Siva and Vishnu of the Gupta period.

The remaining features such as the horns which in one case cover to the front instead of upwards, and the usual holes on each side of the masks for trying or sewing it on, are not relevant here. They might however prove useful in establishing culture contacts with Mesopotamia and other ancient countries in the west. In the third mask the short beard is represented by very shallow incised lines, and is said to be unique among these masks.

Probably such masks must have been found elsewhere, in sites such as Lothal and Kalibangan, but of which we have no idea, as full reports are not available. If they are found, we would very much like the excavators to give the full context of the specimens, if this has been noted on the site.

Conclusion

Though the extent of the great Indus Civilisation or the Harappa culture was being continuously increased in every direction, little evidence was available of its contribution of art history. Important discoveries were made by the Department of Archaeology, the University of Allahbad, and the Deccan College. Professor G.R.Sharma and his colleagues, Dr. R.K.Varma, and Shri Dhaneshar Mandal, discovered a unique bone figurine in the Belan gravels. Shri S.A.Sali obtained fragements in his excavations at Patne, District Jalgaon of an engraved ostrich shell. The discoveries help to span the gap between the Middle Palaeolithic and the Mesolithic with the present brief but connected account, of the birth of the artistic sense and its gradual expression right from the Early Stone Age.

References

Sankalia H.D., *Pre-Historic Art in India*, Kanpur, 1978.

Chandra, Rai Govind, *Studies of Indus Valley Terracottas*, Varanasi, 1973.

Fawcett F., *Notes on the Rock Carvings in the Edakal Cave*, Wynaad, 1901.

Gupta J., *Pragaitihasik Bharitiya Chitrakala*, Delhi, 1967.

Jaida K.P., *Painted Rock Shelters*, 1961 – 1962.

Mitra P., *Prehistoric India: Its Place in the World Cultures*, Calcutta University, 1923.

Wheeler M., *Civilisation of the Indus Valley and Beyond*, 1966.

10

Socio-Cultural Changes under the Portuguese Missionaries on the Coromandal Coast

Dr. R. Krishna Moni

Introduction

The role of Christian Missionaries in stimulating social reform movements and social changes is fairly well known. The Portuguese were the first to impose the alterations of a newly emerging and evolving colonial order in India. The term Christians is a very broad one constituting Roman Catholics, Syrians, Baptists, Presbyterians, Lutherans, etc. Hence delimitation has been imposed; separate identity is spelled out and in this work, one shall deal with Roman Catholics. It is a fact that the Tamil society of a web of inter-relationship that exists among various individuals and social groups of the Tamil country. Society and culture are closely related but both are distinct. The former is the patterns of association and relations through which persons influence or motivate one another, whereas the latter comprises certain products of these regulations in the form of communicable values, norms and standards. Socio-cultural changes had been intensive because the interaction of the Portuguese missionaries was exhaustive.

Portuguese Missionaries

The Portuguese missionaries noticed some common social evils prevalent in the Tamil society on the Coromandel coast and they planned to introduce some reforms. First, they found that several marriages took place between close relatives on the Coromandel coast. Because of the prevailing ecclesiastical prohibition for such marriages, Fr Henriques felt the need to request the Holy See to allow such marriages among the Paravas in the third and fourth degrees of consanguinity and affinity. He thought that it was already much if the Christians could be persuaded to avoid marrying first cousins. Todem and more from these Parava Catholics would be too heavy a burden on them. Thus missionaries were very understanding and initially careful in handling the affairs before introducing any drastic social reforms among the Paravas. Further in several other matters also, the canon law was not enforced among the Paravas. To cite, one may say that the rule of annual confession was not imposed as late as in the year 1558 for the simple reason that there were not a sufficient number of priests to hear the confessions of the people. Those Christians who were guilty of clandestine marriages were punished but only very lightly. The Christian feast days of obligation were made very few. There was also no obligatory feast during the season of lent. The Portuguese had not taken any efforts for doing missionary work on the Coromandel coast from their arrival in India in AD 1498 till the year 1534. Only a few missionaries of the Franciscan and Dominican orders arrived on the Tamil coast to take care of the Portuguese traders.

Francis Xavier

The establishment of the Diocese of Goa in 1534 gave them some space so that a unified missionary enterprise could be undertaken on the Coromandel coast. The Paravas, the fishermen of the Coromandel coast were the first converts by the Portuguese missionaries in 1537. The event of their conversion laid the foundation for the Portuguese pastoral work and their mass conversions also had a great impact on the coastal politics of Tamil Nadu. These new converts retained many of the distinctive features of the earlier social and Hindu religious life. Thus, in reality, the religious conversion of the Paravas initially had not sought much impact on the practice of the Christian religion by the individuals. These details are well recorded in the letters of Francis Xavier. For him, Parava's conversion to Christianity in the Sixteenth century Tamil Nadu meant breaking away from all pre-existing beliefs and social ties. Some aspects of the activities of the Portuguese missionaries in the sixteenth century had been projected in the correspondences and communications of the missionaries of the later period. It is recorded that the Portuguese never understood, in the beginning, the differences between the castes. They never troubled themselves to differentiate between the high and low castes.

They employed freely the Pariahs and the fishermen and made use of them to satisfy their various needs. This conduct of the early Portuguese shocked the natives and they became very prejudicial to this religion. The Hindus considered the people of Europe as a despicable and miserable lot with whom one cannot deal without dishonoring oneself. In another instance, it is stated that the idolaters reasonably perceived the missionaries as persons who wanted to destroy the religion of the country. The Paravas who became Christians declared the King of Portugal as their ruler and the charges leveled on the Christian converts were subjected to forces that denationalised and westernised. Thus one can see how westernisation could be seriously mistaken for Christianity in the sixteenth century. This made the Jesuits of the Madurai Mission successful in evolving an Indian Christian culture that is thoroughly Tamilian and distinctively Christian with a minimum of western influence in the seventeenth century.

Caste System

The word caste is derived from the Portuguese word 'casta' which means lineage. The Portuguese applied the term caste very appropriately having understood the Indian system. In Hinduism caste is referred to as varna meaning colour. Caste in India at that time referred to a social stratification along the lines of descent, which meant an individual born into a given social category remained there for life. Thus caste was inborn and it determined his social status. The rigid system also did not allow an inter-caste marriage. The violation of the rule led to the expulsion from the caste. Many natives who become Christians had been ostracised and boycotted either by the parents or by the family since all marriages were caste endogamous. Thus natives realised that caste was a big obstacle after conversion to survive in the Tamil Christian society. There was no unity among the various castes of Christians who were also divided into right and left-hand castes like the Hindus in Tamil society. The left-hand caste that comprised of drummers, pipers, tom-tomers, Chuckilis, Beri Chettis, Vanniyars, Devangars and Panchalattars, (Kannalars, Kollars, Carpenters) represented an inferior status while the right-hand caste said to be superior status included Mudalis, Pillai's, Komutti Chettis, Kavarai Chettis, Idaiyars, Agamudaiyars, Vellalars, Kaikoalars and Padmasalis. Some of the castes stood for several sub-castes and communities bunched together based on commonage of interests.

It is mentioned in Portuguese records that the Hindus of one caste could not partake of any dish which had been prepared by members of another caste nor drink in their house. This practice continued even among the Christians. The gap between the Christians of low castes and high castes remained wide despite the efforts taken by the missionaries to narrow it down. Since the caste system was tolerated among the Tamil Christians, each caste was allotted a separate place in the church by the missionaries. There was a wall inside the church to segregate the upper caste Christians, Europeans and Eurasians from the low caste Christians. Therefore the wall was removed and the high caste Christians protested. They refused to enter the church for worship. The high caste Christians quarreled with the priests for keeping the proposed church exclusively for themselves. The high caste men came forward even with the suggestion of paying for the priest to serve in that proposed new religious services because the high caste men did not listen to the suggestions of the priests. So they stood outside the church showing their protest. The high caste converts on the Coromandel coastal ways wanted to maintain a distance away from the low castes and the Untouchables. The missionaries were also obliged to give in as they found no way to bridge the gulf between the two. Within the same Church, the communion table and the altar had been common to all although the Pariah Christians and high castes were separated by the pillars and stone benches. Even there were separate doors for entry and exit in the church. The same situation prevailed in many places on the Coromandel coast. Catholic priests had given some concessions to the high caste Christians without totally compromising the egalitarian principle of Christianity. It was felt by the high castes that a considerable concession had been granted to the low castes and the untouchables to have entered into the same church since Hinduism had invariably kept them away from temple entry, the high caste characteristics. Distinct areas were also used for burial and separate cemeteries for the Pariahs existed. Thus, there arose a complex situation and the missionaries had the high task of convincing the high caste Christians that separation between them and the Pariahs would be maintained in the churches. On the other hand, the missionaries also had to convince the Pariah Christians that discrimination would not be allowed in the churches and if at all allowed only to some extent and not permanently. The fear that segregation might be abandoned someday among the Catholics would have deterred the high caste Hindus from converting newly to Christianity. These things had a great impact on the progress of the missionary work and permanently sealed the future of the conversions.

Social Changes and Low Caste Christians

The psychological reactions of inferiority inflicted upon the depressed classes who were not allowed to live in villages nor touch any person of caste or enter the temple were understood by the Portuguese Jesuits. They considered their missionary call to render service in the name of Christ to these low castes. The Karma doctrine in Hinduism that the degradation of low castes was due to their misconduct in the previous birth had to be rejected. Thus the low castes who had no opportunity earlier to respond to the stimulation of nature and environment were attracted to Christian teaching followed by active Christian worship that had been introduced, a privilege which was earlier denied to them by the entry into the temple. Thus 'loving God accessible to all alien to the established Hindu beliefs and the sharing privilege in worship through the removal of social injustice gave a new force into their lives and it became strong enough to loosen and destroy their inhibitions. In the year 1638 when Fr.Martin attended the provincial congregation in Cochin, he had been requested by Fr.Pedro de Basto to concentrate on the conversion of the Paraiyas. It has been generally pointed out by scholars to date that mass conversions of low caste Hindus were taking place. It is equally important to study how the conversion of a single man by change of religion became one of the most incisive events in his or her human life and those who accepted Christianity did not only experience a sweeping change in their own lives but also became carriers of change in the surroundings. There are instances to show in records that they were able to bring more conversions in the process.

Social Changes

The converted Christians also led an exemplary life acting as a catalyst for the spread of Christianity on the Coromandel coast. The Christian religion capable of bringing such a change was felt by them as a true one and the low castes were compelled to acknowledge it.

Thus family as a basis for conversion was felt by the Portuguese Jesuits since they saw the family-like caste as a major force of resistance to Christianity. The Christian missionaries in particular sheltered them and provided them with better living conditions and a better quality of life. There was a change in the converts' way of life but unfortunately, the Christian social order remained more or less the same as the Hindu social order. Normally a convert follows the caste customs and the ceremonies in their life cycle celebrations such as birth, puberty, marriage and funeral. For marriages, every caste follows its custom except for the nuptial blessing in the Church. They also follow the food and dressing habits, of their Hindu counterparts. In some instances, if the converts fail to comply with the caste customs, they were ostracised. Hence the practices of social distance, untouchability and social stratification were not uncommon even among the Christians. The caste system with all its prejudices was not destroyed but was unfortunately prevalent among the Christian converts also. They continued, to be treated by their neighbours as Untouchables and were victims of the same social and economic disabilities as their Hindu brethren of the same category. These Christian converts followed the same usages, customs, manners and habits of life characteristic of each particular caste. The high caste people did not accept the low castes with human dignity and divine grace, and they did not give equality in the churches, cemeteries, schools and village feasts. Social change has received added impetus in the decades before and after the attainment of India's Independence. This is not an isolated trend confined to India only. In every society, changes have been occurring in the social process. It should also be remembered that with the development of modern science, technology and industry, there is a definite swing towards change in the social life of mankind.

Challenges of Reforms

The problem of reform in the context of India is a problem of changing the society from a traditional agricultural society into a modern one. The main problems facing Indian society are the improvement in the poverty of the masses and their standard of living. Confidence and the ability to master the environmental forces, physical as well as social, have to be developed. The poverty of the people is startling. The principal factors which still bind India to poverty are extravagancy and ignorance. The most striking feature of the rural population of India is the absence of a sense of thrift and saving. This fact by itself, together with illiteracy and indifference to change combined to keep the living standards of the people very low. In recounting the causes of waste one cannot leave out of reckoning the large expenditure upon festivals and ceremonies. People expected either God or the Government to make good all their deficiencies. Manual labour was still associated with loss of dignity. Available resources were wasted due to customs and prejudices. The poverty of the Indians sprang from the same roots as the ignorance of hygiene. Excessive adherence to social customs and observances, to the detriment of public health, made the problem of improving sanitation at once so acute and so difficult to solve. With an increase in the receptivity of the classes to new ideas and with the improvement of the social and economic status of the masses, it is hoped that India's backwardness will be remedied. The condition of the untouchables and the depressed classes was still more deplorable. They were subjected to humiliating insults and social disabilities. The persistence of disease combined with inadequate conditions of communication and certain traditional ideas generated the problem. However, the poor cultivator was frequently willing in theory at least to admit that education could improve his material well-being. But it is not easy to convince the people who are daily faced with the problem of poverty and who need the labour of their children, that the ultimate benefit of education was the immediate material sacrifice involved.

Social Problems

Social problems demanding attention were the excesses of intemperance, which sometimes led to violence and crime. The rural folk had a strong temptation for intoxicating drinks and drugs. The drink-evil brought misery to the victim, his family and society. Intemperance had always been held in the highest contempt in the community. The Government policy in this matter seemed 'to take care to minimize the temptation to those who do not drink and to discourage excesses among those who do. Government activities to reduce evil were supplemented by the well-directed efforts of voluntary bodies, especially the Christian missionary societies. These agencies fostered an attitude of mind among the addicts which was calculated to result in permanent improvement. The Catholic Church itself was making decisive efforts to get out of its state of siege mentality and settle down assuming a more positive relationship with the liberal secular culture. Traditionally the Jesuits in the Madurai Mission were involved in evangelisation as their predominant apostolate. The Society itself had been founded for the defense and propagation of the faith and for rendering any service in the Church for the greater glory of God and the common good. The contemporary social and religious trends in the country did not fail to attract the attention of the missionaries. The Jesuits of Madurai were profoundly influenced by the prevailing atmosphere of reform and change around them. The spiritual mission of the Society and its social functions, without being contradictory to each other, fused and enriched each other.

Conclusion

The Mission strategy was therefore to uplift these miserable wretches from economic backwardness and improve their living conditions. As the agents of change, the Jesuits created new and healthy attitudes and values among the people. They prepared them slowly for meaningful participation in their social and religious life. They were made to understand the dignity of labour and the value of hard work. Opportunities were provided at the community level for the people to imbibe positive values. To foster unity among the congregations common sharing and love feasts were introduced. Village festivals and common events of the parishes were made use of to bring the people together. Traditional aspects of culture in the community were properly encouraged. The Jesuits found those village ceremonies were essential to bind the people to the religion and nourish their piety and faith. Superstitious beliefs and faith in sorcery and astrology were the most distressing disorder among rural Christians. All efforts were taken using Parish Associations and intensive instructions to help the ignorant people understand the meaning of their faith. In this way, the Society was trying to reconcile the ways of the tradition-ridden society with dynamic and egalitarian values.

Reference

Albert M. Nevett, *John De Britto and His Times,* Gujarat, 1960.

Antony Raj, *Discrimination against Dalit Christians,* Madurai, 1992.

Azariah. V.S, *Introductory Lessons on India and Missions,* Madras, 1910.

Caldwell. R, *History of Tinnevelly,* Madras, 1881.

Danvers, F. C., *Report on the Portuguese Records,* London, 1892.

Edward Francis, *Man with a Mission, The life of St. John de Britto,* Dindugal, 1993.

Edgar Thurston, *Castes and Tribes of Southern India,* Vol.VII, New Delhi, 1975.

Firth. C.B., *An Introduction to Indian Church History,* Madras, 1968.

Herbert Risley, *Caste and Religion in the People of India,* Calcutta, 1908.

Jean Castes, *The Madura Mission,* Trichinopoly, 1924.

John Correia-Afonso, *The Jesuits in India* (1542-1773), Bombay, 1997.

Kuppuswamy, B. *Social Change in India,* Delhi, 1972.

Money. N., *The Advent of Christianity into India,* Palayamkottai, 1977

Mundadan. A.M., *History of Christianity in India,* Vol. I, Bangalore, 1989.

Nilakanta Sastri. K.A, Development of Religion in South Indian, Madras, 1963.

Rajayyan, K. *British Diplomacy in Tanjore,* Mysore, 1969.

Srinivas. M.N, *Social Change in Modern India*, New Delhi, 1972.

Thekkedath Joseph. C.F, *History of Christianity in India*, Vol. II, Bangalore, 1982.

Thomas, P. *Christians and Christianity in India and Pakistan*, London, 1954.

Stephen Neil, *The Christian Missions*, London, 1965.

11

Portuguese, the Real Founder of the Catholic Christianity in India

R. Navis Abisha

Introduction

Christianity preaches worldwide love and fellowship, as well as benevolent and humanitarian actions. Because of its historical antiquity, it is considered one of the world's greatest religions. According to Pandit Jawaharlal Nehru: "Christianity came to India as early as the first century after Christ, long before Europe turned to it and established a firm hold in South India". South India has churches and relics related with the apostle.

St. Thomas Christian

St. Thomas, one of Jesus Christ's disciples, was a forerunner of Christian missionaries to India. According to Indian legend, St. Thomas arrived by water and initially landed at Cranganore on the Malabar Coast around the year AD 52, when he converted upper caste Hindu families in Cranganore, Palayur, Quilon, and other locations. He also reached the Coromandel Coast, organised the Malabar Christians, and built a few public places of worship. Jordan's book 'Mirabilia Descripta' was written after his arrival in India revealed that 10,000 St. Thomas Christians had converted to Catholicism.

Spread and Growth of Christianty in the World

Christianity flourished throughout the world, particularly throughout the Roman Empire, where it was designated the state religion in the fourth century AD. Later, the church was divided into two large groups: the Western Church, led by the Pope of Rome, and the Eastern Church, led by the Patriarchs of Antioch. The Pope leads the

Catholic hierarchy in the Western Church, which also comprises Cardinals and diocesan bishops. Personal ordinariates and religious groups such as the Jesuits, Franciscans, and Dominicans are part of the Eastern Catholic Churches. The Eastern Church, officially known as the Orthodox Catholic Church, is the world's second biggest Christian church. The Catholic Church, which represents one-sixth of the world's population (18%), has over twenty rites. With the arrival of the Portuguese, Latin Christians first appeared in South India. However, evidence suggests that the Latin Church and Latin Catholics existed in the 13th and 14th centuries.

Latin catholic Christians are like as Roman Catholic Christian. The Roman Church only arrived in India in the 13th century AD. On his trip to China in 1291, a Franciscan monk named John of Monte Corvine stopped in Mylapore with the assistance of a Dominican monk named Big Roae. They were the first missionaries to arrive in India. The Portuguese were the first Europeans to introduce Christianity to India in the late nineteenth century. In the history of India, the second half of the 15th century is characterised by significant voyages of discovery performed by Western European powers. Portugal was one among the forerunners in this venture, which sought to create a new trade route to India and spread of Christianity.

Portuguse, The Real Founder of The Chatholic Christianity in India

The Popes established various agreements with the Portuguese monarch John-II and entrusted them with the job of evangelising the newly encountered nations after seeing his considerable interest and devotion in propagating the Christian faith. The vast lands of southern and eastern Asia were placed under the ecclesiastical jurisdiction of the Portuguese, or Padroado, which meaning Patronage. Vasco da Gama sailed from Lisbon in 1497, assisted by an Arab pilot. On May 20, 1498, he sailed around the Cape of Good Hope and arrived in Calicut on the Malabar Coast. The local monarch, Zamorin, greeted him warmly and sought beneficial commercial relations. Vasco da Gama and his soldiers discovered four ships belonging to Christians who had arrived from Cranganore, and the Portuguese learned of their presence in Melinde. It demonstrates that the Thomas Christians existed before to Vasco da Gama's voyage. The Christians inspired the Portuguese king and instilled confidence in its integrity. As a result, the Portuguese kings were given a say in the nomination of bishops and the dispatch of missionaries. They pledged to give the required donations to the missions and their institutions, as well as to the protection of neophytes (newly converted Christians). They began to provide for the evangelisation of India and other southern and eastern Asian countries by dispatching a number of religious and diocesan priests from Portugal and elsewhere. The Padroado's religious clergy were mainly the same as before, namely Augustinians, Dominicans, Franciscans, Jesuits, and Theatines.

The arrangement between the Holy See and Portugal worked well as long as Portugal could meet her responsibilities. The Portuguese expedition shows that they had two distinct goals: the material one of furthering Portugal's commercial and political interests, and the spiritual one of locating the eastern Christians. Vasco da Gama and his troops encountered no Christians in Calicut or any other Indian port. The four eastern Syrian bishops who arrived in India in 1504 declared in a letter to their Patriarch that the St. Thomas Christians lived eight days' trip south of Cannanore. As a result, the first wave of Portuguese had no interaction with genuine Christians. The Portuguese first made touch with the Christians of St. Thomas in India during Vasco da Gama's second expedition to India. It is learned through the sources of Portuguese chronicles and letters of King Manuel I, King of Portugal at the time of Vasco da Gama and Cabral's travels. Consequently, the Portuguese dispatched a second expedition to create trading centres and expel the Muslims from their ports in the south of Calicut, as well as to build excellent relations with the Portuguese. Thus, the Portuguese would have accomplished both goals: 1. trade interests and 2. Spiritual interests. Cabral's missions were accompanied by & Franciscan Friars, 8 Chaplains, and a Chaplain General, indicating the Portuguese's missionary intentions. Cabral and his soldiers set out from Lisbon on March 19, 1500. They landed in Calicut on August 30 and were warmly welcomed by the king, who granted them permission to build a factory there. To the Muslim merchants' incitement, there were disappointments and tensions between the Portuguese and King Zamora. The Muslims aided Zamorin, and over a long length of time, these hostilities sapped the Portuguese's efforts and destroyed Zamorin's power. Cabral's landing in Cochin was much more momentous than Vasco da Gama's arrival in Calicut three years earlier. Cabral and his soldiers were fortunate to encounter true Christians in the regions.

The historical introduction to the letter of east – Syrian bishops in 1504 was proven in this assignment. "Two Catholic bishops, George and Joseph, arrived in India from east Syria. They were both ordained priests. The entrance of these two bishops invigorated the town with new life. It was the first time they came in Cranganore, the most important religious centre, where the first meeting of the Portuguese and the Christians of St. Thomas took place. Cranganore was the only place in India with a significant population of Christians, and the majority of the residents were Christian and Hindu. With the election of the diocese of Cochin on November 3, 1534, the Latin Catholics' position grew more cemented and well-organised. On February 4, 1558, Goa was elevated to the status of archdiocese, with Cochin Malabar as its suffragan. In festivities, the Greek liturgy was used. These Christians' church fell under the control of a pontiff known as Catholics, 12 Cardinals, 2 Patriarchs, Archbishops, and Bishops. With the introduction of the powerful Portuguese Christians, the Indian Christian community was more strictly regarded by the native authorities. The fresh surge in Christian expansion in India was undoubtedly the result of Portuguese initiative. Portuguese laid a firm foundation for the growth of Christianity in modern India and the encouragement given to inter racial marriages and disregard shown for caste distinction. The propitiatory measures adopted by the Portuguese against certain evil social customs, practices of self-immolation of widows, abuses connected with the devadasi institution, abandoning of children born on an inauspicious days, etc. deserve to be commended.

Downfall of Portuguse in India

The humanitarian actions that effectively communicated the essential message of Christianity were the most striking. However, between 1657 and 1663, the Dutch and English effectively challenged the Portuguese naval superiority in Indian waterways. The Dutch conquered from the Portuguese a number of strongholds and other points of authority on the south Indian coasts, thereby ending the Portuguese influence in those areas. Portugal was no longer able to carry out her missionary duties efficiently after losing most of her trade to the Dutch and English in the seventeenth century. As a result, the Holy See established a new missionary known as

Propaganda and began sending its own missionaries to India and other countries, and Protestantism spread throughout the country.

Conclusion

Theological considerations influenced the concept of missionary service as well. Persons working among the poor have benefited greatly from inculturation in several areas, including theology of liberation, preferential option for the poor, the concept of human rights and justice at the grassroots level, the welfare of the population in times of crisis and natural disasters, particularly women empowerment in Asian culture, which serves as a liberative element for women, Small Basic Christian Communities, and so on. Finally, it is confirmed that "The Blood of Martyrs Is the Seed of Christianity". This was true not only during Roman rule until 1000AD, but also today in all Asian countries. As a result of various intervening political and cultural circumstances, the future of missionary service could develop exponentially and even in-depth.

Reference

George Evers.

Yvon Ambrose, *Mission of the Church in the Past, the Present and the Future in an Asian Perspective*, Pious Association of Jesus the Divine Healer.

Jawaharlal Nehru, *An Autobiography*.

Dinamalar, 6 February, 1986.

Arthur John Franklin, G., "The Impact of Early Christian Church in India," *Journal of the Institute of Asian Studies*, March 2001, Vol. XVIII, No. 2.

Fr. E. Louis Roche, "The Latin Catholic Community in Kerala (1498-1663) Unpublished Ph.D." *Thesis*, University of Kerala, 1989.

NilakantaSastri, *A History of South India*, 1976.

Catechism of the Catholic Church.

Robert S. Ellwood and Gregory D. Alles, *The Encyclopaedia of World Religions*, Infobase Publishing, 2007.

Cyril Bert, *An Introduction to India Church History*, Theological Publications, Madras, 1981.

Hambye. E. R, *History of Christianity in India*, Vol. III, Bangalore, 1997.

Arthur John Franklin published article in "The Impact of Islam on Early Christian Church in India", 1515. 14. Cf. Joseph Wicki, ed. *DocumentaIndica*, 1948, Vol. VI.

The religious priests were the members of different monastic orders, for example, the Franciscan, *The Jesuits and the Dominican Orders who took the three vows of poverty, chastity and obedience.* The religious obeyed their own Superiors

Correa, op. cit, *The chaplains mentioned here were for the spiritual care of the Portuguese.*

Mundadan. A. M., *Sixteenth Century Traditions*, 1970.

Suffragan – denotes that Bishop elected or appointed as an assistant to the bishop or as subordinate to an archbishop or a metropolitan.

Liturgy means a Christian sacrament commemorative the last supper by consecrating bread and wine.

Hambye. E. R, *The History of Christianity form 1542 to 1700.* Vol. II, The Church History Association of India, Bangalore, 1997, Sudir Publications.

'Propaganda' is an office in the Secretariat of the Pope, Rome. This office looks into matters related to faith; regarding the profession of faith and propagation of faith throughout the world.

12

Women's Movement in India

Dr. M. Shyla Kumari

The roots of the Indian women's movement go back to the early nineteenth century when social reformers, beginning with Ram Mohan Roy (1772 – 1833), began to focus on issues concerning women. Roy condemned sati, kulin polygamy and spoke in favour of women's property rights. Improving the condition of women became the first tenet of the Indian Social reform movement. Men who belonged to the socio religious reform associations began the first organisation for women. In Bengal, Keshub Chandra Sen, a prominent Brahmo Samaj leader, started a women's journal and developed educational programmes for women. Members of the Brahmo Samaj formed associations for women of their own families and faith. The Prarthana Samaj in Maharastra and Gujarat did similar work. Narayan Ganesh Chandavarkar, Madhav Govind Ranade and R.G. Bhandarkar in Pune and Mahipatram Rupram Nilkanth and his associates in Ahmedabad started organisations for prohibition of child marriage, for widow remarriage and for women's education. The male-inspired and male-guided organisations for women did valuable work in educating women and giving them their first experience with public work. Swarnakumari Devi, daughter of Devendranath Tagore, a Brahmo leader, and sister of the poet Rabindranath Tagore, who formed the ladies Society in Calcutta in 1882.

In the same year, Ramabai Saraswati formed the Arya Mahila Samaj in Pune and a few years later started the Sharda Sadan in Bombay. The Bharat Mahila Parishad was women's organisations. Women in Calcutta, Bombay, Madras and other smaller cities formed associations.

National Women's Organisation

The early women's organisation had been confined to a locality or city. In 1910, Sarala Devi Chaudhurani, daughter of Swarnakumari Devi formed the Bharat Stree Mandal (Great Circle of Indian Women) with the object of bringing together "Women of all castes, creeds, classes and parties... On the basis of their common interest in the moral and material progress of the women of India". (Bagal, 1964, 24). It planned to open branches all over India to promote women's education. Branches were started in different cities such as Lahore, Amritsar, Allahabad, Hydrabad, Delhi, Karachi and other cities.

Votes for Women

In the inter war years, between 1917 and 1945, there were two main issues that the women's movement took up – political rights for women and reform of personal laws. Women's Indian Association (WIA) was formed in 1917 by Annie Besant, Margaret Cousins and Dorothy Jinarajadasa. WIA was in sense the first all India women's association with the clear objective of securing voting rights for women. A Moemorandum signed by 23 women from different parts of the country, demanding votes for women.

Reform of Personal Laws

The All India Women's Conference was established in 1927 at the initiative of Margaret Cousins to take up the problem of women's education. Women from different parts of India belonging to different religions, castes and communities attended the first session in Pune that was a great success.

AIWC's intial concern was with education but it realised that girls did not go to school because of purdah, child marriage, and other social customs. It therefore took up these issues. It waged a vigorous campaign for raising the age of marriage which led to the passing of the Sarda Act in 1929. AIWC took up the cause of reform of personal law.

Women in the National Movement

Women's struggle entered a new phase with the arrival of Mahatma Gandhi on the Indian Political scene. They had attended sessions of the Indian National Congress and taken part in the Swadeshi movement in Bengal, 1905-11 and in the Home Rule Movement. At the Karachi session of the Indian National Congress in 1930, the resolution on Fundamental Rights gave equal rights to women.

Women in the labour Movement

In 1917 Anasuya Sarabhai had led the Ahmedaad textile worker's strike and in 1920 under her leadership the Majoor Mahajan, the Ahmedabad textile mill workers union was established. Maniben Kara emerged as the socialist leader of railway workers and Ushabai Dange and Parvati Bhore as Communist leaders of textile workers. In the year 1928-29 Bombay textile mill workers' strike, women played a leading role.

The Women's Movement: 1970s to the Present

In post-independent India Women dissatisfied with the status quo joined struggles for the rural poor and industrial working class such as the Tebhaga movement in Bengal, the Telangana movement in Bengal, the Telangana movement in Andhra Pradesh or the Naxalite movement.

Meanwhile in Ahmedabad, what was probably the first attempt at a women's Association (SEWA) at the initiative of Ela Bhat in 1972. Its aim was to improve the condition of poor women who worked in the unorganised sector by providing training, technical aids and collective bargaining. The anti price rise agitation launched in Bombay in 1973 by Mrinal Gore of the Socialist Party and Ahalya Rangnekar of the CPI-M, together with others, mobilised women of the city against inflation.

The Nav Nirman movement, originally a students movement in Gujarat against soaring prices, black marketing and corruption launched in 1974 was soon joined by thousands of middle class women.

The Chipko movement got its name from the Hindi work 'Chipko' which means to cling. This clinging to trees was a particular action people used to save trees, which were crucial to their lives, from being felled. The movement began in 1973 in the small hilly town of Gopeshwar in Chamoli district when representatives from a sports factory came to cut trees. Women joined the movement in 1974 and with their united strength prevented the contractor from cutting trees. It was the women of Chipko who brought to public attention the importance of trees and the need to protect the environment. In the late 1970's, Delhi became the focus of the movement against dowry and the violence inflicted on women in the marital home. Groups which took up the campaign included 'Stree Sangharsh' and 'Mahila Dakshita Samiti' Later, a joint front called the 'Dahej Virodhi Chetna Mandal' (organisation for creating consciousness against dowry) was formed under whose umbrella a large number of organisations worked. The anti-dowry campaign attempted to bring social pressure to bear on offenders so that they would be isolated in the community in which they lived.

Sati was declared a punishable offence in 1829. In 1985 in support of the Supreme Court Judgment in the divorce case where Shah Bano, a Muslim woman, had petitioned the Court for maintenance from her husband under Section 125 of the Criminal Procedure Act and the Court granted her demand. The Orthodox Muslims, however, protested against interference with their personal law. In 1986, the government introduced the Muslim Women's (Protection of Rights in Divorce) Bill denying Muslim women redress under Section 125. Women's associations protested against this outside Parliament.

It was this realisation that has led the women's movement to take up in a more concerted manner programmes of legal literacy and education, gender sensitisation of textbooks and media. The contemporary women's movement provided the impetus for the establishment and growth of women's studies across disciplines. Efforts are being made to prepare reading and teaching material with a feminist perspective. A number of universities and colleges have women's study centers.

Conclusion

The success of the women's movement has not been in the number of women appointed to office or in the number of laws passed but in the fact that it has brought about a new consciousness on the entire question of women in Indian Society. There would have been no women's movement in India if Indian men in the nineteenth century had not been concerned with modernising women's roles. They focused on certain issues such as sati, child marriage, condition of widows, education etc. Women came out and created a space for themselves. They started organisations of their own, first at the local, then at the national level. They were motivated by liberal feminist ideas and the belief that education, granting of political rights, and legislative reforms would improve women's position. They fought for the country's freedom and believed that independence from foreign rule would remove obstacles in women marching forward. In the second phase, the women's movement was more radical and challenged patriarchy. History shows that though the struggle for women's rights is long and hard, it is a struggle that must be waged and won. The Women's movement thus has a long way to go in its struggle for bringing about new values, a new morality and a new egalitarian relationship.

References

Omvedt, G (1993) *Reinventing Revolution: New Social Movements and the socialist tradition in India*, New York.

Oommen, T.K. (1993) *protest and change: Studies in Social Movements*, New Delhi: Sage Publications

Rao, M.S.A. (ed.) (1978) *Social Movements in India*, Delhi: Manohar Publications.

Sarkar S (1983) *Popular Movements and Middle Class Leadership in Late Colonial India Calcutta:* Centre for Studies in Social Sciences.

Touraine A., (1977) *Self Production of Society,* Chicago: University of Chicago Press.

13

An Insight into the Colonial Sway in Katharina Kakar's *Moving to Goa*

Archana N. S and Dr. Sheeba. S. Nair

Katharina Poggedorf Kakar, better known as Katharina Kakar is a Goa based writer and artist. Apart from being a writer and artist she also runs an NGO 'The Tara Trust' providing education for deprived children. Kakar has also served as a lecturer, executive tour-guide, free-lance project assistant and museums guide in various countries. In her writings she deals with the aspects that address the changing global landscape of identities. Kakar calls herself as a cultural "bridge-builder", who understands herself and others within shifting realities. She has to her credit three books namely *Women in India, The Indians* and *Moving to Goa.* The chosen work *Moving to Goa* is a travelogue, exploring the history of Goa and the debates and fissure that engage and divide Goan society today. It gives an insightful look at Goan society and portrays Goa with all its paradoxes and problems, its seductive pleasures and unique enduring charm.

The term Colonialism means an act of gaining full or partial control over other country, through brutal subjugation of indigenous people. According to a history expert Robert Longely "colonialism is the practice of one country taking full or partial political control of another country and occupying it with settlers for purposes of profiting from its resources and economy" (ThoughtCo.). Colonialism existed from the ancient period, when a particular civilisation extended its borders and established colonies by drawing people and population resources.

The modern colonialism began with the advent of Portuguese in the fifteenth century, when the Portuguese explorers set sail in search of new trade routes. Vasco da Gama landed in Calicut through Cape of Good Hope and a new sea route from western Europe to Asia was discovered. Goa being a defensible island with excellent harbour facilities on either side attracted the Portuguese explorers towards it. As a result, Afonso de Albuquerque, the Portugal soldier conquered Goa and it served as the Portuguese headquarters for four and a half centuries. As the goal of colonising countries is to make profit from the human and economic resources of the colonised countries, Goa soon became an important trade hub for the Eastern spice trade. Ships from the port sailed across the empire from East Africa to Japan bringing in horses, spices, slaves and other goods which was of importance.

As Goa became a hub of activity, attracting people from different parts of the world, its external influences also intensified.The colonial influences include some of the elements like religion, language, culture, architecture and political practices. When some countries are badly affected by the colonial influence, there are some settlements which have been benefitted by it. For instance, Singapore attributes its "impressive economic development" as the "valuable aspects of colonial heritage" (ThoughtCo.). Colonisation has helped the underdeveloped and developing countries to boom in many fields. Goa is one such place, which attributes its impressive heritage to the colonial rule. The present paper unfolds the influences, which blends Goa into a rich cultural heritage and attracts tourists from various parts of the world.

Christianity and the church play a dominating role in the coastal belt. Christianity was introduced to Goa by the Portuguese. It is believed that Lord Parashuram created Goa by shooting an arrow into the sea and the portion of land till the sea retreated, formed the Konkan coast. Before the arrival of Portuguese, the natives were all Brahmins. But with the arrival of Portuguese, the temples were destroyed and the suppression of Hindu faith was in full swing. Many temples were destroyed and churches were constructed in its place. Katharina Kakar in her travelogue *Moving to Goa* mentions that,".. . the main church in Benaulim, named after the St John the Baptist – an impressive building founded in 1581 – was originally constructed at the site of a temple for Benespur or Benespor, the Lord of Arrow, close to the shore" (58).

Mother Mary in her many different forms seems to be so much important than Jesus to most Goan Catholics. The reason behind this is that, the cult of the Hindu mother goddess was very strong in Goa before the Portuguese inquisition. Mother goddess was worshipped in her various forms. Kakar notes that, "She was worshipped as

Santeri (Goddess of the Anthill), Mauli or Shantadurga" (84).When large scale conversions are made from one religion to another, it is reasonable that not everyone understands the new religion in its own terms. Instead, the people attempt to understand it in terms of their old religion. Therefore, the Portuguese started giving more importance to Mother Mary and introduced various feasts like the annual procession of Our Lady to persuade Hindus to convert to Christianity. Katharina Kakar notes that she has,".. . never seen or heard of 'sleepover parties' of church statues anywhere else in the Christian world" (80). Therefore, it can be noted that the tradition of carrying Mother Mary to every house is also a Portuguese influence.

The arrival of the Portuguese in Goa changed the face of its architecture. Initially the imported designs of buildings did not well suit the climatic conditions of Goa. However, with time the masons craftmanship were shaped by the European ideals, infused with their understanding of the local context. Therefore, around eighteenth century a distinct style of architecture emerged which include mouldings, decorative features and embellishments and intricately designed railings. This can be commonly seen in the house of elite Goan Catholics even today. Katharina Kakar in her travelogue *Moving to Goa* describes one such mansion owned by Dona Maria Lourdes Figueiredo – Albuquerque, an elite Catholic from Loutolim.

The mansion gave a sense of stepping into a time wrap with its grand staircase, flanked by lush lawns and flowering shrubs. The mansion was decorated with exquisite mosaic flooring in patterns of birds and dogs. Kakar puts it as: "The library, ballroom, salon and dining hall, the private chapel within the mansion, collection of delicate porcelain, a profusion of carved rosewood and oyster shell windows letting in a lovely translucent light – all these are typical features of these mansions, mirroring the life of the Portuguese – Goan elite of the nineteenth century" (69). This house is a part of Goa's cultural heritage and is in collaboration with the Xavier Centre of Historical Research, converting it into a vibrant living museum that evokes a vanished era. Similarly, another house in Quepem, the Palacio do Deao, located on the banks of the Kushavati riveris renovated with eighteenth century antiques. It now serves a villa for people who want to witness the grandeur of Portuguese era and taste Indo-Portuguese cuisine. The houses and lanes are kept very clean in Goa. During the Portuguese rule it was mandatory to paint the house every year after the monsoons. This practice has been evolved as a tradition among Goans.

The churches and cathedrals of Old Goa are all built based on the Portuguese style. The famous seminary in Goa, "The Rachol seminary" (60) was built by Diogo Rodrigues, an explorer, who later became the captain of the Jesuit seminary. The seminary with its beautiful library lends its service to the society and has helped in the development of Konkani literature. Katharina Kakar describes the place as, "The Rachol seminary, where the Catholic clergy is trained even today, has a superb library and enough antique furniture, relics and paintings to furnish a whole village" (60-61). The author also mentions "The Patricinio Chapel" (61), situated in Benaulim. This chapel was built in 1805, in Portuguese style and has a beautiful whitewashed façade with the priest's house near it.

Apart from the architecture, religion and the rest, Goa's colonial past left an indelible mark on its cuisine. The new culinary practices were rooted in traditional dishes and ways of cooking. The unique cuisine of Goa developed out of a merger of various cultures that came into contact with over the centuries. A classical example of Portuguese influence on the food of Goa is that the cuisine includes vinegar, which is otherwise an uncommon ingredient in traditional Indian cooking. Vinegar helped to preserve food in a time when there were no refrigerators. Goan vinegar is special, since it is made from the sap of the coconut palm tree. Katharina Kakar notes the major difference between Hindu and Christian cuisine as, "One of the most apparent differences between Hindu and Catholic food is in the use of vinegar – it is taboo in Hindu cooking, but an essential ingredient in many Catholic dishes, such as vindaloo, balchao, or sorpotel" (110).

Bakeries were introduced by Portuguese. Therefore, most of the bakers in Goa are Catholics. Bread was used in Goan diet even before the arrival of Portuguese. But the coming of Portuguese brought with them a distinctive variety of bread called "pao" (111). The arrival of Portuguese replaced "canjee" (112), the traditional Goan breakfast with pao. Today, Goan people wake up to the horn of bread man. Katharina Kakar notes it down as:

> The squeaking horn of the bread man as he carries a basket full of *pao* (Goan bread rolls) and cycles through the village lanes, wakes up all the households in our neighbourhood with its loud and persistent *poin-pum*.... Whether eaten with butter and jam for breakfast or dipped into a hot

> lentil-and-vegetable curry, the Goans love their pao and often have it at lunch or dinner as well. (111)

Cashews play an important role in Goa, since it is used to make "feni" (7), a native liquor of Goa. The journey of cashew in Goa began when the Portuguese brought in the cashew plant from Brazil to prevent soil erosion and to increase the forest cover. Today native drink is brewed out of cashews and consumed by the natives in the same quantity as water. Most of the other vegetables and fruits and flowers were introduced to Goa by the Portuguese. Few other things introduced to Goa by Portuguese are potatoes, chilies, guavas, tomatoes, pineapple, pineapple and different kinds of meat. Katharina Kakar wonders,

> ...how Goan villages in the coastal belt, now dominated by the Catholic Culture, would look if the Portuguese had never conquered Goa. No churches, no pigs; saris instead of dresses; maybe not even tomatoes, potatoes and chillies, since these vegetables introduced by the Portuguese (as so many other plants), took a very long time to be accepted into Hindu cooking. (64)

Inspite of the rest, the colonial rule did introduce some enlightened laws beneficial for women. During 1559, when the wives, widows and girl children in the rest of India could not inherit land, houses and immovable possessions, the Goan women had access to it. This law helped Goan women to have self-confidence and be independent. Moreover, the Portuguese passed laws which allowed widows to remarry. Under the rule of Portuguese, the women had access to education as well. Moreover, nunnery was introduced by Portuguese. The famous nunnery Santa Monica was built in 1606. The convent grew to be an important educational institution. Today, there are many convents in Goa and the nuns do admirable work to help the poor and the vulnerable in the state.

It can be noted that colonial inquisition was not all bad, but beneficial in many ways. In fact, many Goans cherish the colonial period and are dissatisfied by the liberation and post-Liberation period. As Damodar Mauzo remarks, "many Goans felt after Liberation that the governance of their state was in the hands of wrong people" (214). According to him the corruption and negligence is because the government is mainly run by people from other states who are not aware of the treasures of this beautiful island. The people of Goa have no control over their state's development. In the words of Maria Lourdes Figueiredo –

Albuquerque "Goa was not liberated,... it was invaded by the Indian army!"(67).

It can be concluded from the above influences that Goan culture is a product of centuries of intermixing of various influences and stands to be the best in many aspects. For instance, Portuguese architecture has evolved as the best tourist attraction in Goa. Old Goa is a paradise of distinct churches and cathedrals shaped in Portuguese style. Goans, despite their differences manage to coexist as one community. This melting pot of different customs and traditions is reflected in the daily lives of the people, where different communities take part in each other's festivities, rituals, theatre, food sports and many more.

References

Cartwright, Mark. "Portuguese Goa." *World History Encyclopedia*, 11 June 2021, worldhistory.org. Accessed 12 Aug. 2022.

Kakar, Katharina. *Moving to Goa.* Penguin Random House India Pvt. Ltd, 2013.

Longley, Robert. "What Is Colonialism? Definition and Examples." *ThoughtCo.*, 16 Feb. 2021, thoughtco.com. Accessed 14 Aug. 2022.

"Portuguese India." *Britannica*, Britannica.com. Accessed 28 July 2022.

Raut, Mohit. "An overview of Portuguese colonial architecture in India." *Rethinking the Future*, re-thinkingthefuture.com. Accessed 10 Aug. 2022.

Silveira, Lester. "The Balcao, Goa's Beloved Porch." *Paper Planes*, 6 Dec. 2021, joinpaperplanes.com. Accessed8 Aug. 2022.

14

History Silhouetted in the Culture: A Critique on Duong Thu Huong's *Paradise of the Blind*

Chitra K. S.

Literature in its broad sense is a body of creative writing recognised especially of artistic and intellectual value, often due to deploying language in ways that differ from ordinary usage. Literature can be classified into fiction or nonfiction and poetry or prose. It can also be distinguished based on the major forms such as novel, short story or drama. Literary works are also often categorised according to the historical periods or through their adherence to certain aesthetic features or expectations. History according to the Merriam Webster dictionary is the branch of knowledge that records and explains past events. People of the upcoming generations get to know the details of the past not only through those historic documents and through the people who witnessed it in the past. Here literature also plays a major role in digging up the events that took place years ago. History of a particular place or a group of people, the background they lived in, the problems that shattered them down, how they rebuilt themselves from their downfall all these details can be known through the writings of various writers in a fictional way. There are so many works that help people to understand the dark periods, how people suffered a lot to title their problems and survived hard to set everything back to normal in the land they lived in.

Duong Thu Huong is a Vietnamese author and political dissident. She was born in the year 1947 in Thai Binh, a province in Northern Vietnam. Her parents were Duong Dinh Chau and Ngo Thuy Cham. She was a member of a revolutionary family and a member of the communist party. She was also a part of the Ho Chi Minh generation. Duong studied at the Vietnamese Ministry of Culture's Arts College.

She was an active leader who volunteered to serve in the women's youth brigade on the front line of the war against Americans. In 1979 when China attacked Vietnam, she became the first woman combatant who stood on the front lines to witness the conflict. She was the vocal advocate of human rights and democracy. She led the next seven years of her life in exile, hiding herself in jungles and in the tunnels of Binh Tri Thien, the most heavily bombarded region in the war. Her mission was to sing louder than bombs. She focused on giving theatrical performances for the North Vietnamese troops, burning the dead and accompanying the soldiers along. She was one among the three survivors out of the 40 volunteers in the group. Duong became highly outspoken and critical about the repressive atmosphere created by the communal government. She was expelled from the communist party in 1989. She was also imprisoned for more than half a year as the result of her political beliefs.

Though she was one of Vietnam's most popular writers, almost all her works were published outside Vietnam due to the issues with the censorship hand because of the government's monopoly of the publishing industry. She says that most of the writers must learn how to voice their individual concerns with the group mentality. She also suggests that the writings of a writer must reflect the individual in him and the masses at large in the way which is approved by the party; she finds that most writers in contemporary Vietnam get caught up in the group thinking mentality. She herself is a victim of censorship. Duong herself has felt the effect of censorship more cruelly than many of her fellow writers. It is a bitter fact that none of her works are contained in any Vietnamese anthologies or collections. Though she is successful in creating various works, which were meant to be read by her own audience in Vietnam, they often do not have the opportunity to read her work, except when it is smuggled through Vietnam. She is nevertheless hopeful for the future of writing in her country. She keeps on counting on the fact that at some point the people in Vietnam would open their eyes and look at all the brutalities which are going on around them in their homeland without her help. After her imprisonment, Duong worked mostly as a translator in Vietnam to earn her livelihood, while publishing her novels and short stories abroad. She was then made a Chevalier of the Ordre des Arts et Des Lettres by the French government in the year 1994. In 2005 sea earned the PEN award which recognises writers who have been persecuted for their work. Duong moved to Paris in 2006 and lives there currently.

Duong's first novels, *Journey in Childhood*, *Beyond Illusions*, *Paradise of the Blind* and *The Lost Life* were published in Vietnam and soon became the best sellers in Vietnam before they were banned. Most of her works focus on the themes like beauty, culture, family, freedom, identity, poverty etc. Duong's work *Beyond Illusions* is a disturbingly powerful work known for its depiction of totalitarianism. Through this work she offers memorable portraits of 1980s Hanoi introducing through three characters who all face moral crises about the way they live. The order becomes too honest to discount the political implications of their situation. In her other work *Memories of a Pure Spring,* she continues to criticize the injustices of the communist party by focusing on their country's performing artists. Duong uses a confusing divided narrative to explore the interrupted careers and embattled marriage of eminent composer Hoang Hung and his wife Suong, a patient girl from the mountains of Central Vietnam who's in net musical ability earns her fame. The writer presents a series of flashbacks within flashbacks discussing the early life of the little girl and her decision to leave the home in order to become a singer. Suong gets arrested and undergoes great suffering in the prison. In another work titled *Novel Without a Name,* in 1995 the writer deals with the story of a young commander who struggles to find his identity in the confusions of the last days of the Vietnam war. Through this work, Duong portrays Vietnam's long and bloody war for independence and socialism. Most of her works explore not only the political realities of post war Vietnam but also the quest to find meaning in daily life through art and love. Her last novel *No Man's Land* won the Grand Prix Des Lectrices De Elle award in the year 2007.

Duong's novel titled *Paradise of the Blind* was one of her best works and it was also the first Vietnamese novel ever published in the United States in English. This is her fourth novel and the fourth one to be banned by the Vietnamese government. The story of the novel *Paradise of the Blind,* is set around the life of Hang, the protagonist of the novel. The novel is narrated in flashbacks as the protagonist is on the train to Moscow. When the novel begins Hang lives in Russia as an exported worker. It was at that time she received a telegram from her angle informing her about his sickness and asking her to visit him in Moscow. Hang doesn't want to go because they do not share a close relationship with each other and moreover she herself has just recovered from her illness. During the travel the protagonist remembers the incident when her mother Que told her about her father Ton for the very first time. Hang gets to know only a few events that took place before her birth through her mother. Hang was only 9 years old when her uncle visited them after a very long time. He insisted on Que to take up a job as a factory worker saying that she is now being a part of the exploiting class as she works as a vendor. Que has sold their ancestral house and Uncle Chin asks Que to give him his share. Que says that she would collect it back from the village and bring it back to him. When both Hang and Que go to their village, they meet Aunt Tam there. Aunt Tam gives them a great feast and later on during the feast both Que and Hang get to know about the aftermath of Rectification of Errors and they also get to know about the death of Ton through Aunt Tam.

Que and Hang stay for a week in the village and when they leave to go back to their town Aunt Tam gives the little girl food, gold earrings and two rings to take back with her. When the festival of Tet falls, Aunt Tam visits them in Hanoi to give Hang a huge amount of food for the New year's celebration which she says is "an offering to Ton's memory". The little girl starts to notice that since she met her aunt, her mother had become more distant from her. When Que hears that her brother is sick, she goes to meet him where she meets his wife and his two children. When she notices that they don't have much to eat she sends her daughter to their house the next day with a large amount of food. Hang becomes frustrated thinking that her mother is doing much for her uncle and his family who doesn't even care about them. When Tet comes, Que again sends food to her brother's house, not even taking care of her daughter's immediate needs.

As years pass, Aunt Tam once again brings a large amount of food for her niece during the festival of Tet. Que, who expected the arrival of Tam, decided to spend all her money on buying food for her brother and his family rather than on her own family. Hang then goes to the Institution of Social Sciences for her higher education. Back on the train the protagonist recalls a year prior when her uncle demanded for her to come to Moscow for the very first time. She had bought him a suitcase of goods which he then traded on the black market. Que starts to save money for her brother and her brother's family when he was diagnosed with diabetes by cutting the amount spent on their own food. Hang loses a substantial amount to the point where she suggests selling a ring that her aunt gave her, so that they can eat.

The next day Aunt Tam visits them and she learns about the situation. Things start to degenerate between mother and daughter until one day when daughter confronts her mother about lying to her aunt. Que kicks her out of the house. One day Hang learns from her neighbor that her mother was hit by a car and that her legs have been amputated. Sheer wheels that are why she had moved to Russia in order to work there and to support her mother.

The story now moves to the present where the protagonist arrives in Moscow and finds that her uncle is no longer in hospital. It was only on the next day she realised that her uncle had called her to get money from her and to help him by selling his goods in the black market as she speaks fluent Russian. When Hang returns to the dormitory, she receives another telegram informing her that her aunt is dying. Hang goes to her aunt's house and finds that she is very frail. When Aunt dies, Hang arranges for three memorial ceremonies for her but decides not to live in the house which was given to her as a token of legacy. The novel ends on a note where the protagonist thinks that she cannot waste her life keeping up the legacy of the past times and she dreams of returning back to the university auditorium and traveling to another spot where a planes could land and take off.

The story focuses on the life of three women – Hang, Que and Tam fighting to maintain dignity under a government that discards old values and tears families apart. Even though her mother's love pulls the protagonist down, she pulls herself up and finds liberation in choosing her own path and pursuing a life that will make her happy – because her duty to her mother, who would sacrifice her own daughter to help her corrupt brother, is not her happiness. She decides to choose her own path of happiness, not letting herself to be a toy in the hands of fate.

Food culture can be defined as the attitudes, beliefs and practices that surround the production and consumption of food which incorporates our ethnicity, culture, heritage and provides a mechanism of communication with others both externally and within our families and communities. The likes and dislikes of people on food varieties depend on the surrounding in which they live and the place in which their ancestors originated. Food is seen as something that is more than that of mere means of survival. According to

Roland Barthes, "food is described as a system of communication, a body of images, a protocol of usages, situations and behavior. In other words, food sums up a situation constitutes information and becomes a sign and unit of a system of communication when one buys an item of food or consumes it" (29). In that aspect, Duong Thu Huong in her work *Paradise of the Blind* brings in the most striking element and constant discussion of food throughout the novel.

Huong uses vivid images to describe the traditional foodstuffs. The novel stresses on the significance of food in Vietnam and its enrichment as an aspect of Vietnamese culture. It also emphasizes the Vietnamese deep cultural connection to the love of food. Their reverence for food is reflected throughout the novel. Food not only reflects and expresses potential identity in life and in literature, it also mirrors cultural identity and escapable of creating boundaries and differences between the cultures. It also plays a major role in digging up the history of the people. The novel uses food as a powerful weapon of human expression. It also plays a major role in quantifying one's love, respect or even hatred for another human being. The famous Vietnamese saying "A morsel of food is a morsel of shame" throws light on the belief that giving or accepting food reveals once status in the hierarchy of the social order. It also deliberates the role of food in various aspects resulting in drastic changes in the life of the characters which paves way for the development of the plot of the novel.

The elaborate explanation of Vietnamese food not only depicts the cultural and social aspect but also clearly portrays the deep inner thoughts and entrenched love that the protagonist has for her homeland. Food becomes a recurring theme and plays a significant role throughout the development of the plot of the novel. Food also plays a vital role in bringing to light the past events that happened before the birth of the protagonist and how it has affected her in her present life. By depicting the problems in the life of the protagonist, Huong also makes the readers understand how those incidents that took place in the past affected the lives of the natives in Vietnam.

Huong in *Paradise of the Blind* uses food as a medium to communicate various things such as culture, tradition, love for each other, reminder of the past events that took place in Vietnam etc. It is when Que and Hang go to Hanoi to their aunts house for the very first time, Aunt Tam serves them with a huge variety of traditional food items. It was at that time, while they were having their food Aunt Tam informs Que and Hang the aftermath of Rectification of Errors which resulted in the suicide of Ton, Hang's father. Here we get to know the history of Vietnam. *Paradise of the Blind* takes place between the 1950s and 1980s in Vietnam. Until the 1950s Vietnam was under the control of the French from the late 19th century. In 1945 communists and Vietnamese nationalist combined under the leadership of Ho Chi Minh, who declared Vietnam independence and ultimately won the Gorilla war for independence in 1954. Vietnam was then divided into North Vietnam and South Vietnam. North Vietnam became a communist state under the support of the Soviet Union whereas South Vietnam became a noncommunist state backed by the US. During the period between 1953 to 1956 the North Vietnamese government took a great decision which affected the life of many people. The project was a land reform campaign. The effect of this land reform is mentioned as the background of the novel *Paradise of the Blind.* The land which was privately owned was redistributed to over 1.5 million farmers and peasants. As a result of this thousands of villagers were arrested and nearly 1 lakh farmers were forced and sent to labor camps as the result of the court law because they were viewed as being part of a higher land-owning class. After a year, the government understood that the land reform campaign which they undertook was an utter failure. And it has cost the lives of millions of people and has become the major reason for the widespread social unrest in the nation. In order to eradicate this mistake committed by the government, the government itself undertook another campaign named "Rectification of Errors". As a result, the people in the camps were sent home and allowed to reclaim their lands. This is the background from which the entire novel is built up.

In the novel *Paradise of the Blind*, Duong brings in the history of Vietnam in an elaborate manner and keeping it as the background, she has painted out beautifully the lives of the characters and how the history of Vietnam has brought twists and turns in the life of the characters. Though Duong doesn't go deep on the politics of the war, it was Ho Chi Minh's leadership that garnered support and ultimately led to Vietnam's liberation from France. Uncle Chinh is the most vocal supporter of the Communist Party, featured in the book. After the death of Que's parents, she led a life of loneliness until she met Ton. Her brother was completely running behind the

Communist Party. Que tells Hang how she spent her days feeding herself meagerly with "a hardboiled egg on a tiny plate. A clear soup with a few springs of bindweed plucked from the hedge. Life was all around me, but it was life that belonged to others" (20). Later on, the relationship between Ton and Que develops which was not at all liked by Chinh. Chinh explains to Que that Ton's entire family are landlords, who are bitter enemies of the peasant class. He says "that the party is about to begin land reform, and the Ton's family are the people who they must condemn and punish" (33). When the land reform campaign started, Ton and his family lost all what they had and were dragged down to poverty where they had to beg someone for a meal a day. Ton leaves the country. Que and Ton were no longer husband and wife. Que begins to deteriorate physically and mentally, Uncle Chinh tells her to stop grieving on Ton and his family. Six months later Uncle Chinh leaves to join the Land Reform section and Que too bundles up her baggage and leaves the village.

Months later Que returns to the village, the Rectification of Errors begins. This campaign was started by the government to rectify the land Reform which had wrought immense problems and suffering. People talk about the injustice they suffered. The entire people of the village march to the house of Que, in search of Uncle Chinh whom they believed to be the cause for all these problems. However, Aunt Tam intervenes telling them that Que had already lost her husband at the hands of her brother and does not deserve more punishment than this.

Years later Que and Hang return to their village and meet Aunt Tam, who serves them a huge banquet. The inside of the house is just as extravagant as the outside, and Hang is even hesitant to sit down. Aunt Tam offers them a spread of food that rivals a Tet feast. It is at that time through Tam, Hang gets to know that her father has committed suicide. Tet, short for Tet Nguyen Dan, Spring Festival, Lunar New Year or Vietnamese New Year is the most important celebration in the culture of Vietnam. The people in Vietnam celebrate this festival annually, which is based on the lunisolar calendar. Vietnamese people who live far away usually return to their families during this festival. Some return to worship at the family altar or visit graves of their ancestors in their homelands. They also clear up the graves of their family members as a sign of respect. They prepare a large amount of food as a part of the celebration. First of all, food is important in the worship of their ancestors. Secondly, it is for the reunited family. And lastly, it is to welcome visits from friends and guests. All these forms a part of Vietnamese culture. The entire neighborhood of Hang celebrating this festival and everyone preparing Che pudding and sharing it with their loved ones also portrays the connection between food, culture and community. Food acts as a means of retaining their cultural identity. It helps to bridge the gap between people. Thus, food plays a major river in portraying the culture of Vietnam.

Aunt Tam, Hang and Que go outside for tea in the Courtyard and there she serves them tea scented with jasmine flowers. She also reminds Que that her wedding tea was also scented with jasmine which grew on the wall of their house. Here food imparts nostalgia, bringing back the beautiful memories from the past. Aunt Tam speaks about how during the land Reform they divide the house into half. She also shares her experience when she worked as a hired labor in the village and how she gradually learned to make duckweed into the floor and noodles. Aunt Tam said she "knew how to make vermicelli noodles out of river weed" (77). She added that she also invented a machine that would grind the duckweed which she could buy for nothing and sell for a lot more. She was a hard worker who;

> After a week of experimenting, I invented a machine that ground the duck weed by crank. I did everything by myself and when I sold the noodles at the village market, I made a quite tidy sum. At that time that weed cost me next to nothing so I bought two tons. Filled the house up with it. There wasn't a corner left to hang my hammock in. So, I slept on the mat in the temple courtyard. I kept every penny I earned in my belt and slept with the knife under my neck (77).

In this context food serves the purpose of being the source of survival and livelihood. Aunt Tam, who did not have any means to lead her life after the land reform, tries her level best in the work in which she is good at. Has she known the art of making noodles from river weed, she uses it as a means to support her living, thus uplifting har livelihood to a better and higher level. She also grows paddy in her field. It also resulted in gaining her reasonable profits. Here Duong explains how food has become an inevitable factor in the development of Tam's life after the land reform.

This paper History Silhouetted in the Culture: A Critique on Duong Thu Huong's *Paradise of the Blind* focuses on food playing a major role in various contexts throughout the novel both in depicting the past life and culture of the Vietnamese through the characters in the novel. Although the imagery of food may have many different meanings throughout the novel, it signifies one's social status in Vietnam society as well as the care and affection of family bonding. Food in the novel stands as a symbol for human expression and also as an expression of one's personal value. Foods like a significant measurement that measures one's love, respect and hatred for people and the environment around them. The warmth caused by the love and care between family members is also expressed through the medium of food. The novel further showcases the significance of food in relationships through Hang and her mother's cyclical relationship. Either in the case of gifting or showing hospitality, for instance, the offers come through food. The treatment and descriptions of food in the novel vary shortly depending on the setting and fully reflects the protagonist's feeling of both isolation and alienation, as well as contentment and resentment. Thus, Duong Thu Huong has used rich and tasty images of food in various contexts in various aspects to reflect the growth, degeneration of characters, to remind the past events, to understand the culture and tradition and also to understand the bond between characters in the novel.

References

Huong, Duong Thu, Duong, Phan Huy and McPherson, Nina (Trans). *Paradise of the Blind*, HarperCollins Publishers, 2002.

Barthes, Roland. Counihan, Carole and Esterik, Penny Van (ed.) "Towards a Psychology of Contemporary Food Consumption." *In Food and Culture*. New York, 2008.

https://www.encyclopedia.com/arts/educational-magazines/duong-thu-huong 1947,23 December 2022.

https://www.sd5.kl2.mt.us/userfiles/54/my%20files/land_reform_in_vietnamese _literature.pdf?I'd=1826, 02 January 2023.

15

A Historical Study of Siva Temples in Cheranmahadevi Taluk – A Study

Dr. V. Manikanda Sethupathy

Introduction

Cheranmahadevi is a very tiny portion While comparing with the extent of land moss of India. However, it Possesses a large Population and stands as a Place that reveals tradition and culture. It has a long history from Sangam Age. Cheranmahadevi has a district Place in the history of Tamil Nadu also[1]. In ancient days the land was not full of rocky and useless for cultivation. Due to land reclamation, the land in and around the administration of all the three kings who rule Tamil Nadu.[2] The history of the country or the part of the country naturally becomes the part and parcel of the history of the kings who ruled it. History is nothing but the mirror of the past. It becomes true here. Today history is being reviewed in a multi-faceted manner. Researchers undertake their tasks to Probe the history along with varied branches of study. Once, the history of man and the history of Politics were distinct branches. Today, the system has been reversed. We undertake research either separately or combined on Social, economic, cultural, religious, philosophic, literature, and artistic values aspects. Social History Is a Separate Branch. When individuals join together it becomes family and the families from the clan.[3]

History of Cheranmahadevi

Hence, it is imperative to chalk out the history of the village for the purpose of not chalking out the history Country. Gandhiji rightly pointed out that the root of India is the root of villages. There is a separate system to review the history of the village or the clans. Following the system, I put forth the review under the head and caption of "History of Cheranmahadevi". The Perennial river

Thamirabharani flows through Cheramahadevi which makes the entire landscape greenish.[4] "Chadurvedhi Mangalam" was its original name. It is understood from the stone carvings. It is said that Cheran Kovilpatthu was the location of the castle of the Northern entrance and south entrance, besides Shencottiyan sathan, a Malayala deity was also found here. These stand as evidence that the town was under the reign of Cheran king[5].

The ancient history sounds well in the name of this town. This town stands in the name of Mahadevi of a Cheran in the Southern part of Pandiya Kingdom, we understand that grew the heredity of a Cheran King[6].

In ancient days, Cheranmahadevi was the border town of Chera king Udhaya Marthandavar. At the time of the marriage of his daughter "Mahadevi" to Pandiya king, he gave this town to him as a dowry. And thus history reveals that this town is known as "Cheranmahadevi" thereafter.[7]

Temples in Cheranmahadevi

As Religions are an inseparable force in Indian culture. There are six major temples and a hundred minor temples of recent origin in Cheranmahadevi.[8] The major temples belong to the Chola, the Pandya, and the Nayak dynasties. Among the six temples four namely Ramasamy temple. Naduviliappan temple, Appa temple, and Bhaktavatchala temple are dedicated to Vishnu and the remaining two namely[9]. Ammainatha temple and Deviysvaramudiyer temple are dedicated to Lord Siva, all indicating the peaceful coexistence of Saivism and Vaishnavism. It is interesting to note that these temples stand for different sects of Hinduism namely Saivism, Vaishnavism, Ganapathiam, Kaumaram and Saktham. The Presence of the temples in Cheranmahadevi stands as a testimony to the religious unity which is the characteristic feature of Hinduism in India[10].

Cheranmahadevi is one of the oldest holy centers in Tamil Nadu. The temples of Cheranmahadevi has made a unique contribution to constructing the religious, social, and political life of the past and present people. These temples of Cheranmahadevi also supply the various valuable inscriptions which serve as authentic evidence to construct the history of the early Pandyas Cholas ad later Pandyas who were the ruling class of the ancient and medieval period of South India.[11]

Besides the innumerable temples dedicated to the minor Gods and Goddesses one at least of which presides over each separate colony. Ammainathasami temple Cheranmahadevi is one of the foremost temple of Nava Kailasam temples situated on the northern and southern banks of river Thamraparani at papanasam, Cheranmahadevi, Kodakanllur, Kunnathoor, Murappanadu, Srivaikundam, Thenthirupperai, Rajapathy and Sernthamangalam.[12] The other names of the temple are Kailayattanar temple. Cholendrasingaiswaran temple, Rajathi Raja Tiruchchurailai. Kailayamudaiyamahadevar temple and Ammainathaswami temple is one of the biggest temples in the Tirunelveli district of Tamil Nadu. It is located on the southern bank of river Tampraparani and is 2.40kms away from the Cheranmahadevi. Like many other big temple of south India this temple was not built all at one time but was the result of many centuries of growth and development.[13]

Where Lord Siva adorns as ThingalGraha in Navakailayam. Cheranmahadevi is situated in the Southern riverbed of Tampraparani is surrounded by beautiful greenery that appears like a green carpet. The presiding Deity is Sri Ammainathar alais Kailayanathar and Goddess Avoodainayaki (Amman). There are two big gates and a small Raja Gopura on the east. Lord Ammainathar is concerned on the northern side and Goddess Avudaiammai on the Southern side of the temple.[14]

Lord Ammainathar himself originated from and adorns the place. In the temple, Nandi and Flag mast are found. Inside the temple Mandapa, Dwarabalagas and Nandi have been consecrated. In the South, Lord Nataraja with Goddess Sivagami and Goddess Karaikal Ammai.

Surya and Chandra are West-facing in the temple. There is a gate South – facing and a Mandapa in the East. This Mandapa is in a precarious condition with damaged pillars. The sculpture of sage Uromasa who worshipped Lord Siva, is seen on a pillar inside the temple. The devotees here pray sage to uromasa also.

The scenes of two ladies who crush paddy and have a Muram are seen on the South side. On the western side of the temple are seen Lord Kasi Viswanathar and Goddess Visalakshi and on the North Western side are seen Lord Subramanya, Valli-Deivanai, and Gajalakshmi, Saneeswara, and Chandeswara.

The History of this Temple

Sage Uromasa Munivar reached the Kailaya Mountain and at the foot of the Banian tree worshipped Lord Siva and prayed for immortality. Historical facts reveal that the sanctum of Lord Ammainathar temple was built by two sisters. Those sisters were saving money to build the sanctum by paddy-crushing work. They were not able to save enough money to build the sanctum through this work.

They were much worried about this and prayed to Lord Siva. Lord Siva went to the house of these two sisters in the disguise of a Brahmin. The two sisters put a leaf in front of Him and served food. At that time there was no light in the house. So the Brahmin said that he would not eat in a house without light. Immediately the sisters bought oil and lighted the candle and served food. Lord Siva, in disguise of a Brahmin, had food and wished the sisters and left the house.

From that day, there was prosperity in the house of the sisters. History says that the sisters together erected the sanctum in the temple. The sculpture of two sisters crushing paddy is found on a pillar in this temple. This is proof for the event. There are stone inscriptions to show that Raja Raja hola and Rajendra Chola built this temple. The name Cheranmahadevi is seen in the stone inscriptions.

Ammainathaswami temple as, it stands today is vast and impressive complex of structures enclosed by high and massive compound walls all around occupying as a rectangular plot of land.

Siva Temples

Except for Ammanthasamy temple and Deiviwaramudaiyer temple, Vaithiyanathaswamy, oppilanayaki temple, Ekambaranathar Kamatchi Amman Temple. Kasiviswanather Visalakshi temple. Somanathar Somasundari Ambal Temple, Sokkanathar Meenakshi Temple, Thonthantrinathar Kameswari temple and Sundaraswara Meenakshi Ambal Temple are situated in Cheranmahadevi.

Vaithiyanatha Swamy Temple

This temple is situated on the southern bank of Kannadiyan Canal just in the western side of Cheranmahadevi Bus Stand. The idol in the sanctum-sanctity is called Sivaperuman Vaidhynathar. Umaiyammai is called Oppilla Nayaki.[15]

Vaidhyanather Perumal seen in the from "SIVALINGA" in the sanctum-sanctity. Next to him "PALLIYARAI CHOKKAR" is kept. Eight Nayanmars, Sugathever, Thakshinamoorthy, and the young Pillaiyar are also seen there. Vaidhyanatha Peruman is seen jointly with oppilla nayaki together with four small Lingams, three Ambal, and Lord Murugan with Deivayanai.[16]

In the temples of this town, there are numerous stone carvings. Totally about 141 stone carvings are discovered in the temples. A stone carving dated back Sagam 1522 Kollam Year 774 when Sadavarman Thirapuna Charavarthy Kulasekara Thevan was ruling the part had been found on the eastern side of the wall of Madabam of this temple quoted the appointment of Viswanathea Naicker as an Accountant by the President Krittinappa Naickar.

The Ammainathaswami Temple

It is located on the southern bank of the Tamraparani, in the northeast corner of Cheramadevi, about 16km south-east of Ambasamudram. Facing east, this temple dedicated to Siva, ad its tritala imana is built of stone still yalivari and of brick above that. It has a large number of epigraphs belonging to the periods of Rajaraja I and his successors as well as their viceroys who were in charge of the Pandya province. From the earliest record issued in the twenty-third renal year of Rajaraja I, it is considered that this temple might have come into existence around.[17] Besides this epigraph, certain architectural and sculptural traits of the monument also support this dating. The temple has two parts. North Part is known as Ammainathar Temple. The southern part is known as Auvudaiammai Thiruthali. Lord Ammainathar appears to be Moorthy who emerged automatically in the Sanctum-Sanctum. The sculptor was not made with a chisel. The figure of Uromasa Saint is found on a pillar in the Mani Mandap of this temple who founded temple. There is the peculiar story behind the construction of this temple.

Arulmigu Ammainatha Swamy jointly Arulmigu Auvudaiammal Temple is known as the "Second Named Nine Kailash" which is situated in Cheranmahadevi.[18]

The Ramasvami Temple

Rmaswamy Temple is situated beautifully on the north part of this town. It has a long past history. Inside the Sanctum-Sanctrum, the God Adhinarayana Perumal and the Goddess Sri Devi and Poodevi are seen there. His holy image is invisible, i.c. no idol from. The structure is water is waterproof. He roof above Him is double-story. The super-structure known as Vimanam" of this temple has its own beauty. It is most artful. Though it is very old, yet very attractive and artful. One of the kings of Cheramahadevi constructed this building with a view to providing a safe place to the people of this place during wartime.[19]

This temple is situated approximately four furlongs (0.80km) to the south of the Tamrparani in the heart of Cheramadevi town, nearly 16km south-east of Ambasamudram. The triala vimana of this east-facing Vishnu temple is built of stone up to yalivari ad of brick over that. On the evidence of an inscription issued in the twenty-fourth regnal year of Rajaraja I, the Ramasvami temple may be placed around A.D.1009.[20]

There is no historical background of its location i.e. "STHALA PURANA" its ancient place is the ancient old village. Brahmins are residing here. They were all brought here by Kritinappa Naicker and each of them was gifted with an acre of land. The Principal God of this temple is the Adhi Narayanan who resides in the sanctum-sanctrum of this temple. Festivals were conducted for him only. The elderly people of this place say that about 150 years ago the idols of Lord Ramaswamy, seethe and Lakshmanan was recovered from the wells located in the kitchen and thereafter prominence was given to Lord Ramaswamy and the temple was known, Ramaswamy Temple.[21]

The Stone Carvings numbered 179 to 184 available in this town belonged to this temple. Out of these, some revealed about Ghee-lamps and some about land-gift (Bhoodhan). Tery is found on the walls of south and North. Carving No.180 and 183 say about the period of kopparakesari Panmaran Rajendra Chozha Thevar. Carving No.184 says about the devotional verse of Thirunantha Lamp by Sri Rangam, daughter of Sri Rangathu Nintrum Ponthu erunga Paradesi Ammaiyaril Andinar.

Art and Architecture

Tamil Nadu is a land of temples, big and small, spread throughout the State. Though these temples are primarily centers of worship and religion, they have many historical and art historical dimensions of which architecture is one of the most important aspects, since it provides a wide scope to study and analyze the plan, elevation and details of the temples of distinctive dynasties in different regions and ages.[22] The study of temple architecture also helps us to understand how the variegated architectural components of the temples underwent development, experimentation, influence, mutual exchange, and standardization due to various factors in different chronological phases under distinctive dynasties. This chapter presents an elaborate account of the plan, elevation and the details of twenty-one structural temples of Cheranmahadevi taluk belonging to the periods of the Early Pandyas, Cholas, and the Medieval and Later Pandyas from the ninth to the thirteenth century A.D. These twenty-one structural temples, on the basis of their dynastic affiliation and chronology, have been divided into the following four groups i) Early Pandya ii) Chola iii) Medieval Pandya and iv) Later Pandya.[23] The architectural characteristics of the temples in each group have been analytically and comparatively studied to understand the development of temple architecture in this particular micro-region under various dynasties and chronological phases in relation to other contemporary monuments found outside the research area.

Sculpture of the Temples

In the Hindu temples architecture and sculpture are two inseparable entities like the body and the soul. Since the sculptures are an integral part of the temples, their study is inevitable in any temple architectural research. The sculptures with their different mudras, hasthas, asanas, ayudhas, vahanas and bhangas have a message for the onlooker.[24] The sculptures in the temples also provide a variety of concepts, themes and the myths found n Hindu religious literature. They also shed light on the dress, costumes and fashions of the bygone times. This chapter attempts to analyze the forms, iconographical details and stylistic characteristics of the stone sculptures available in the temples of cheranmahadevi taluk under study.[25] Like architecture, the sculptures in the temples of the research area, on the basis of their dynastic affiliation and chronology, have also been classified into four categories, namely Early Pandya, Chola, Medieval Pandya and Later Pandya.

Conclusion

Chenmahadevi is a favorably located area in Tirunelveli District. It is gifted to be situated on the banks of the river Thamirabharani. It is greenish everywhere agriculture is Predominant here. The property of this area invites people from other places to settle down here People following various cultures and religions live here together happily. As there is good economic development in this area, the

People lead a prosperous life. Many people are working in sun Paper Mill. They are also engaged in agriculture, mat making and weaving. People following different religions are living together with fraternity and equality. People of this area treat everyone as their kith and kin. Religious tolerance is prevalent everywhere and in everyone.

Cheranmahadevi is teeming with temples to the extent of calling it as a "Temple City". Due to lack of maintenance and renovation, the ancient temple are found in dilapidated conditions. The Government should take necessary steps for the upkeep of the temples and thus they should be made worthwhile to conduct poojas according to Hindu tenets. For a long time, cheranmahadevi was under the influence of Pandyas of sangam age, Pandyas of Madurai, Pandyas of Tirunelveli and the Pandyas of tenkasi. As Kokai served as the ancient headquarters of the pandyas. Cheranmahadevi brought under the influence of pandyas highly. The history of Pandya rule into the cheranmahadevi region began onwards. After korkai, Madurai became the place of Pandyas. The present research shows that the temples under study are located either just on the river banks or near the rivers or away from the rivers. Most of the Early Pandya and the Chola temples and some of the Medieval Pandya temples are situated on the river banks or near the rivers whereas almost all the Later Pandya temples are located about 1 to 2km, away from the rivers. From the study of the spatial distribution of these temples, it is understood that the most fertile areas immediately adjoining the rivers were first colonized in the Early Pandya, Chola, and the Medieval Pandya periods, while the vacant areas lying away from the rivers having wet and dry lands were next inhabited during the later Pandya epoch.

End Notes

1. K. R. Srinivasan, *Temples of South India*, New Delhi, 1985, p. 123
2. K. V. Soundara Rajan, "Early Pandya, Muttarayar and Irukkuel Architecture",
3. Architecture ed.Pramod Chandra, New Delhi. 1975, p. 257.
4. G. Subiah, *Early Pantiyan Architecture,* Unpublished Ph.D. Thesis, Calcutta University, Calcutta, 1977, p. 252.
5. Michael W. Meister (ed.), *Encyclopaedia of Indian Temple Architecture: South India: Lower Dravidadesa*, Delhi, 1983, pp. 122-23.
6. S.I.I. Vol. XIV. no. 13
7. S.I.I. Vol. XIV. no. 36
8. K.V Soundara Raajan, *Indian Temple styles*, New Delhi197 P.119

9. Sthala varalaru The Tirumulanatha Temple at Ambasamudiram, and Devisvaramudaiyar, Appan and the Bhaktavatsala Temple at cheranmahadevi
10. A.R.E. 1916, No.640,
11. SII.VoL.XIV, No.190, pp.104-105.
12. Pandian. T.B., *The Ancient Heroes of south Indian, Peninsula, madras*, 1893., p 152.
13. A.R.E. 1916, No.629.
14. Vithuvaan Perumal, K.V., Porunai Valam, Chennai, 1977, p.77.
15. Arulmigu Vaithiyanatha Swamy Kovil Thala Varalaru, 1999.4-6
16. ARE., 1916, No.640SII., Vol.XIV, NO.190, pp.104-105.
17. ARE., 1916,No.626.
18. ARE, 1916, No.618-B.
19. Arulmigu Ramaswamy Thirukkovil Varalaru, 199, pp.4-6
20. E.I Vol. No.6, pp. 46-47.
21. ARE 1895, No0183.
22. Arulmigu Ammainathaswamy Thirukovil Thala varalaru, kovil Veliyeedu, Cheranmahadevi, 1999, pp.3-7.
23. Arulmigu Ramasamy Thirukovil Thala varalaru, kovil Veliyeedu, Cheranmahadevi, 1999, pp.3-4
24. G. Subiah, *Early Pantiyan Architecture*, Unpublished Ph.D. Thesis, Calcutta University, Calcutta, 1977m p. 252.
25. Parameswaram pillai.V.R, Temple culture of south India, Trivandrum, 1985, p 85.

16

Pilgrimage Tourism in Madurai with Special Reference to Meenakshi Amman Temple

Dr. D. Uma

Introduction

Pilgrimage has been defined as a journey resulting from religious causes, externally to a holy site, and internally for spiritual purposes and internal understanding[1]. Temples are considered as a place of worship, as well as a Centre for religion and cultural activities. They play a multifaceted role in the religious, social and economic life of the people. India is rich in pilgrimage centers like Varanasi, Badrinath, Ketharnath, Both-Gaya, Jaganath Puri, Golden Temple, Mount Abu, Meenakshi Amman Temple, Rameswaram and countless others. Besides Hindus, Muslims are the most prominent religious group and they are an integral part of Indian Society.

India's glorious traditions and rich heritage are closely linked with the development of tourism. Its magnificent monuments attract a large number of visitors from all over the world. The wealth of cultural traditions extending over thousands of years, the natural surroundings, the architectural masterpieces, the music, dance, paintings customs and languages – all these go to make India a tourist paradise. Few countries in the world provide such varied interests to a visitor.

In the words of Nehru, India is "a land of contrasts", where rural tranquility rubs shoulders with metropolitan bustle, austerity with pomp and show and pageantry with simplicity. History has been equally generous in bequeathing a treasure of monuments. There is the immortal Taj, the Dravidian temples of the south especially those of Madurai, and the world famous frescoes of Ajanta and Ellora.

There is also no dreath of cities that create an impression on the tourist.[2] Madurai is a treasure – chest for the foreigners who are keen on knowing about the religious life and tradition of the Hindus. Madurai, known as the Temple city, is one of the important pilgrimage centers of India. It is an ancient pilgrimage city in Tamil Nadu, situated on the banks of the river Vaigai and an important railway junction. It is about 490 Km from Chennai and 458kms by road. The city attracts a large number of pilgrims from within India and abroad. This city is also known as the festival city. It is considered as cultural capital and a great seat of learning since time immemorial. This study makes an attempt to find out the important religious places in Madurai and trace the importance of Meenakshi Sudareswarar Temple as a pilgrimage Centre.

Meenakshi Amman Temple

Known as 'Koil Nagar' (the temple city), this city is a sacred centre with the world famous Meenakshi Sundareswarar temple. The temple is dedicated to Meenakshi, a form of Goddess Parvathi, and Sundareswarar, her consort, God Shiva. The Meenakshi shrine is one of the 51 Sakthi peetams and this Sakthi Peetam is called as 'Rajamathangi Syamala Peetam'. The idol of Amman is made of Emerald. This temple is first among 366 temples which are in the name of "Meenakshi Sundareswarar temple".[3] This temple is hailed as the seat of Budhan (planet mercury). Goddess Parvathi incarnated herself as a mortal, reigned as the Pandyan Princess and married Lord Shiva. A distinct feature of Meenakshi in terms of iconography is the presence of parrot in her right hand. In the Meenakshi Sundareswarar Temple importance is given to Goddess Meenakshi than Lord Sundareswarar as Meenakshi is considered as the queen of Madurai and Lord Sundareswarar as the son-in-law.

Structure of the Temple

Meenakshi Sundareswarar temple is located in an area of approximately 17 acres and the outer walls of the temple form a rectangle, 847 feet by 792 feet[4]. Immediately within the wall are the Adi streets and running around the temple just outside the wall are the Chithirai streets. Outside the Chithirai streets are the Avani Mula streets and then the Masi streets, which enclosed most of the built-up area of the city until at least the mid-eighteenth century. The outer most Veli streets run alongside the line of the old city's fortified walls, which were demolished in the early nineteenth century by the British. Hence the basic grid of the city, which is still clearly apparent, is defined by a set of concentric squares around the great temple at the centre, whose axis of orientation lies almost east-west. The geometry of this scheme is further emphasized by the streets aligned with the four principal gopuras of the temple. The lofty elegant towers of these gate ways structure punctuate the urban skyline, dominating the life of the city.

The Meenakshi Sundareswarar temple is a vast complex containing 12 gopuras of varying sizes, two vimanas, a beautiful tank, numerous mandapas with fine pillars and an abundance of fine sculptures in stone and in mortars. Essentially it contains the two important shrines of Lord Sundareswarar and of Goddess Meenakshi. Of these the Sundareswarar shrine is the older, going back to the legendary times. The Meenakshi temple adjoins the Sundareswarar temple and stands to the south of the Sundareswarar shrine. The sanctum of the Sundareswarar shrine is a squre structure, the exterior walls measureing 33 feet on all four sides. The Meenakshi shrine and its prakarams are smaller than those of the Sundareswarar shrine. The sanctum sanctorum is almost a square measuring about 25 feet each side with the ardhamandapam on its front. The architectural features of the Meenakshi sanctum seem to indicate that it may belong to the first half of the Vijayanagar period about the 15th century[5]. Apart from the towers and two vimanas there are numerous smaller shrines to other deities. Many prakaras, gopuras, mandapas, corridors, doors and staircases were added along with sumptuous grants, offerings endowments etc. by the rulers. Sri Meenakshi temple is compared with human body – Ashta Sakti mandapam as leg, Veda mandapam as ankle, Meenakshi Nayakkar Mandapam as thigh, Dark Mandapam as waist and Golden Lilly tank as stomach and so on.

It is a convention in this temple, different from that followed in other temples, that the devotees offer worship first to Goddess Meenakshi, Therefore, while there are four other entrances into the temple, under large gopuras in the four cardinal directions, it is customary to enter not through any of them but through the Ashtasakthi mandapa, with no tower above it.[6] This entrance leads to the Goddess.

The depiction of dancing Nataraja with his right foot raised is a unique feature of this temple. The hall where Nataraja is said to have danced is known as Velliambalam or Rajatha Sabha or Silver Hall.

Gopurams

Gopuram is an entrance building oblong in plan rising up into a tapering tower of pyramidal shape over 45-50 meters in height and entered by a rectangular doorway in the centre of its long side. It marks "the stage of transition between the effluent maturity of the Cholas and the exquisites though extravagant production of Vijayanagar."[7] A soaring upward sweep which, although not entirely substantial is very impressive.[8] There are twelve Gopurams in the Meenakshi temple. All the outer *gopurams* are nine storeys high reaching a height of nearly 150 feet each, the tallest being the southern tower, 51.9 metres high. There are also two golden Vimaana over the Sanctum of the main deities.

A detailed examination of the four outer gopurams of the Madurai temple would show that though they maintain the general scheme of kutam, pancaram and salai as on most of the Dravidian gopurams, yet their style of ornamentation differ to some extent thus revealing subtle changes in their evolution. They differ from each other in a minor key but in their overall size and shape they are in consonance.

Outer Gopurams

Sl.No	Name of the Gopuram	Name of the Builder	Year	Height (in feet)	Basement Length & Breadth (in feet)	No. of Stucco Sculptures
1	East Gopuram	Maravarman Sundarapandyan	1216-38	153	111/65	1011
2	West Gopuram	Parakrama Pandyan	1315-47	154	101/63	1124
3	South Gopuram	Siramalai Seventhi Moorthy Chettiar	1559 AD	160	108/67	1511
4	North Gopuram (Mottai Gopuram)	Krishna Veerappa Naicker	1564-72	152	111/66	404

Lotus Tank

Lotus Tank or Pottramarai Kulam is situated within the temple complex. It was in this pond that the Golden Lotus for Indra to perform his puja bloomed. It was here, that the plank of Sangam appeared and established greatness of the moral text called Thirukkural[9]. In keeping with the boons granted by the Lord to a stork, upto this date neither fish nor is other life found in this miraculous sacred pond. Since this theertham was created before all other theerthams it is called Adhi Theertham

Mandapams

The temple has enormous number of mandapams like Ashta sakthi mandapam, Veera Vasantharayar mandapam, Kilikoondu mandapam, Kalyana mandapam, Unjal mandapam, Kambathadi mandapam, etc. A striking feature of the temple is the astonishing structure known as Ayiramkal Mandapam or the Hall of Thousand pillars and each pillar features high, ornate, bold sculptures that look life like. View from any angle these pillars appear to be in a straight line, an architectural masterpiece. On the ceiling near entrance is a 'Chakram' or wheel giving details of the cycle of 60 years of the Tamil Calendar.[10] In the outermost corridors are situated the matchless musical pillars carved out of stones. When it is tapped each pillar produces different musical note. Since 1966, the thousand pillars hall is also doubling as the museum of the temple where icons, photographs, drawings and other exhibits are preserved.

Meenakshi Amman Temple has a fine collection of Jewels which are invaluable. Among them a pendent donated by the Pandya king, a head dress studded with gems, pearls and diamonds presented by King Thirumalai Nayak, a 108 sovereign chain by the East India company and a pair of golden stirrups presented by Collector Rous peter are to be mentioned. The temple jewels are used to decorate the deities during the festivals and other auspicious days.

Festivals

Festivals are celebrated in all the months of a year. Chithirai festival is celebrated with same joy every year which attracts lakhs and lakhs of devotees. Vasantham festival, Unjal festival, Aadi Mulai kottu festival, Avani Moolam festival, Navarathri festival, Theppotsavam, etc., are some important festivals celebrated in the temple. Chithirai

Brahamostavam, Meenakshi Cornation, Meenakshi Thirukkalyanam and Temple Car Procession are the important events in the Chitirai festival. Thousands of people visit Madurai from very distant parts of India.

Allazhagar's entry into River Vaigai

This festival is a separate celebration that was celebrated by Vaishnavites. Azhagar went to river Vaigai to redress the curse of Mandooka rishi and, as per Mandooka's wish he showed him all the ten avatars of Lord Vishnu and blessed him. During the rule of King Thirumalai Nayak both the festivals were merged as one single event to unite the people of two groups (Saivism and Vaishnavism). Since then this is celebrated as one grand event during the Tamil month of Chitirai and this gives the celebration its famous name Chitirai Tiruvizha.

Thiruparankundram Subramanya Swamy temple

Thiruparankundram is 8 Km away from the city. This place is mentioned in the sangam literary work Thirumurugatrupadai as the first abode of Lord Muruga. Ahananuru, Maduraikanchi, Kalithohai and Paripadal also mention about this place. The traditional legend is that Murugan, son of Lord Shiva, married Deivanai at Thiruparankundram which also is the first among the six Holy Abodes of Murugan (Arupadai Veedu, literally Six Battle Camps). This evocative cave temple is much older and has a more sacred atmosphere than the Meenakshi temple.

Paran + Kundram became Parankundram. Paran denotes Lord Shiva. Tevaram songs mention this temple as Shiva temple[11]. It is believed that this cave temple existed much before 6th century and was converted into Jain Shrine under the patronage of Pandya king Koon Pandya. Later it was again converted into a Hindu temple by Gajapathy a Pandya minister in 8th century. The main shrine has separate cells that house the sanctums of Murugan, Durga, Vinayaka, Shiva and Vishnu. The deities are carved on the walls of the rock. A special feature of this temple is that the images of Shiva and Vishnu are carved facing each other.

Kudal Alagar Perumal Kovil

Besides the Meenakshi Amman temple, there are few others of minor importance. The chief of these is the Perumal Kovil, situated in the south-western part of the city. This beautiful Vishnu temple has Navagraham also (usually Navagraham is found only in Shiva temple). It is one of the 108 Divyadesam dedicated to Vishnu, who is worshipped as Koodal Azhagar and his consort Lakshmi as Mathuravalli. It appears to have been patronized by the Nayak kings who were Vaishnavites. The architecture of the temple, in spite of modern innovations, deserves study on account of the light that it throws on the growth and development of the ancient Dravidian architecture.

Immaiyil Nanmai Tharuvar Temple

The temple is dedicated to Shiva in the form of Nanmaitharuvar – the Bestower of Benefits – is situated close by to Meenakshi Amman temple[12]. The Sthalapuranam says in regard to this temple, that Madurai was once threatened with floods, the God saved the city and had a temple built by the king.

Alagar kovil

Alagar kovil is a celebrated Vishnu temple 21 Kilometres northeast of Madurai situated on the foot hills of Solaimalai. The deity Kallazhagar, is believed to be the brother of Meenakshi, the presiding deity at the Meenakshi temple the festival calendars of these two temples overlap during the Meenakshi Thirukalyanam festival[13]. The architecture of the temple attracts tourists

Pazhamudhirsolai

Pazhamudhirsolai is located 21 km away from Madurai. It is one among the 6 abodes of Lord Muruga, called as Arupadaiveedu, being Thiruparankundram as the first one. On the top of a hill with forests around, it is quite close to the Alagar kovil. Lord Muruga is seen here with his two divine consorts Goddesses Valli and Deivayanai. Many devotees come here for wedding, child and even academic blessings. The scenic beauty of the place also attracts many visitors here.

Thirumohur

This temple is a Vishnu temple dedicated to Kalameha perumal. It is 11 km from Madurai near Melur. It is one of the 108 Divyadesam dedicated to Vishnu and glorified in the Divya Prabandham. The shrine of Chakrathalwar is one of the attractions for the visitors.

Thiruvathavur

Thirumarainathar Temple is a Hindu temple dedicated to Lord Shiva at Thiruvathavur. It is located 9 Km from Melur in Madurai District. The temple is situated on the northern banks of river Vaigai. The place is considered as birth place of Manickavasagar, the great Saivite poet.

Kazimar Big Mosque

This famous mosque is located at the heart of the Madurai city, within 500 metres of the Periyar bus stand and 800 meters south west of the Meenakshi temple. His Holiness Hazrat Kazi Syed Tajuddin, a descendant of Prophet Muhammad, who came from Oman during 13th century, received this land from the then Pandya king, Koon Pandya and constructed the mosque which is the first Muslims' place of worship in Madurai[14]. Madurai Maqbara, the dargah of famous Madurai Hazrats is also located inside the mosque premises. It is the oldest Islamic place of worship in the city.

Gorippalayam Dargah

A beautiful green coloured tomb can be seen from the AV.Bridge Madurai, which is the Gorippalayam Dargah located in the northern banks of river Vaigai. The name Gorippalayam comes from the Persian word Gor which means Grave. This area is called as Gorippalayam because the Graves of the two famous saints of Islam and rulers of Madurai Hazrat Sulthan Alauddin Badhusha and Hazrat Sultan Shamsuddin Badhusha are located here. It is amazing to see that, the dome which is 70 feet in diameter and 20 feet in height is made of a single block of stone which was brought from the Azhagar Hills.[15] People from all over Tamil Nadu come here to seek blessings and go back fruitfully.

St. Mary's Cathedral Church

St. Mary's Cathedral in Madurai is the seat of the Roman Catholic Archdiocese of Madurai. It is one of the oldest Roman Catholic churches in India and situated 2 km South East of Madurai Railway station and 200 meters from the Thirumalai Nayak Mahal[16]. Its architectural beauty attracts many tourists along with its religious importance.

Suggestions and Conclusion

Madurai is an important religious centre not only for the Hindus but also for the Muslims. Thiruparankundram has become a symbol of religious harmony among the people of Madurai. An Islamic Dargah is located at the top of the hill, where the grave of an Islamic saint is found. Irrespective of religion, people from all parts of Tamil Nadu and from Kerala visit this Dargah. For the promotion of religious tourism in Madurai the following suggestions may be followed.

- The infrastructure facilities can be improved.
- Guide services can be developed to all the religious sites.
- A religious tour package service within Madurai can be promoted.
- Transport facility to connect all the religious sites can be provided.
- Religious handbook on religious sites can be provided to tourists.
- Basic amenities, cleanliness, hygiene and medical facilities have to be developed.

Madurai is popularly known as Thoonga Nagaram meaning the city that never sleeps, on account of the active night life. The city attracts a large number of tourists from within the country and abroad. About 9,100,000 tourists visited Madurai in 2010 including 524,000 foreigners. It has a well transport facility by all means of accessible for tourists The National and state highways passing through the city connect various parts of Madurai district. Madurai Junction is the major railway station serving the city. Madurai airport offers domestic flights to some cities in India and international services to Colombo, Dubai and Singapore on daily basis.

The distinct features of the Meenakshi Amman temple attract the pilgrims not only from all over India but also from other parts of the world. Even a casual visitor is fascinated by the many features and sculptures of this temple. There is an assessed 33, 000 sculptures in the temple and it was in the list of top 30 nominees of the 'New seven wonders of the world'. Meenakshi Sundareswarar temple gleams as a diamond in the crown of the city of Madurai.

References

1. C. Aruljothi, S.Ramasamy, *Pilgrimage Tourism Socio-Economic Analysis*, MJP Publishers, Chennai, 2015, P.7
2. A. K Bhatia, *Tourism development Principles and practices*, Sterling Publishers Pvt. Ltd, New Delhi, 2009, P.307
3. VSV, Arintha Alayankal Apurva Thagavalkal (Tamil), Vikatan Pirasuram, Chennai, 2008, P.14.
4. N. Pandurangan, Ariyappadatha Madurai (Tamil), New Century Book House Pvt.Ltd., Chennai, 2018, P.10
5. Thiruppanimalai V.22 says that the Amman Sannidhi, Maha mandapam, first prakaram and palliarai were built by Thirumalirunjolai Mavali (1452 AD)
6. N. S.nRamaswami, *Temples of South India,* Maps and Agencies Publications, Madras, 1984, p.145.
7. B. N. Luniya, *Evolution of Indian Culture*, Educational Publishers, Agra, 1951, P.271.
8. Percy Brown, *Indian Architecture*, Taraporevala Sons Co. Private Ltd, Bombay, 1953, P.107
9. Opcite, N.Pandurangan, P.4
10. K. Palaniappan, Koil Managar (Tamil), K. Thiagarajan, (Trans), *The Great Temple of Madurai,* Arulmigu Meenakshi Sundareswarar Thirukkoil, Madurai, 2012, P.97
11. P. Rajendran & C.Santhalingam, Mamadurai (Tamil), *Pandiya Nadu Historical Research Centre,* Madurai, 2015, P.120
12. Madura A Tourist Guide Illustrated, *Asian Educational Services*, Madras, 1991, P. 122
13. Sanjay Singh, *Madurai The Madhurapuri*, Sunjoy Publisher, Agra, 2018, P.251
14. Rajesh Singh, *Pilgrimage Tourism*, Sonali Publications New Delhi, 2017, P.190
15. Ibid. P.192
16. Ibid. P.194

List of Contributors

1. **Archana N. S**, Part-Time Research Scholar, Assistant Professor and Research Guide, Register No: 22123184012006, Department of English, Sree Ayyappa College for Women and Research Centre, Chunkankadai, (Affiliated to Manonmaniam Sundaranar University Abhishekapetti, Thirunelveli, 627012).
2. **Chitra K. S.**, Net Apirant, Nagercoil.
3. **Dr Pradeesh S.**, Assistant Professor, Iqbal College, Thiruvananthapuram.
4. **Dr. Anand Lali Seena**, Assistant Professor of History, Sree Ayyappa College for Women, Chunkankadai.
5. **Dr. D. Lekha,** Associate professor of History, Sree Ayyappa College for Women, Chunkankadai.
6. **Dr. D. Uma,** Head & Assistant Professor, Department of History, Mannar Thirumalai Naicker College, Madurai-4.
7. **Dr. D. Vinoba Gladis**, Assistant Professor of History, St. Mary's College (Autonomous), Thoothukudi – 628 001.
8. **Dr. G. Subbiah**, Head & Asst. Prof., P.G. Dept. of Economics and Research Centre, S.T. Hindu College, Nagercoil.
9. **Dr. Hari krishnan P.K.**, Asst. Professor, Kerala Institute of Tourism & Travel Studies (KITTS), Residency,Thycaud, Thiruvananthapuram.
10. **Dr. M. Shyla Kumari**, Assistant Professor of History, S.T.Hindu College, Nagercoil, Kanyakumari District, Tamil Nadu.
11. **Dr. R. Krishna Moni**, Assistant Professor, P.G. Department of History, Khadir Mohideen College, Adirampattinam, Thanjavur.
12. **Dr. S. Doral**, Assistant Professor of History, S.T.Hinducollege, Nagercoil.

13. **Dr. Sheeba S. Nair**, Assistant Professor and Research Guide, Assistant Professor and Research Guide, Register No: 22123184012006, Department of English, Sree Ayyappa College for Women and Research Centre, Chunkankadai, (Affiliated to Manonmaniam Sundaranar University Abhishekapetti, Thirunelveli, 627012).
14. **Dr. V. Karthik Nisha**, Assistant Professor of History, Sree Ayyappa College for Women, Chunkankadai. Kanyakumari District.
15. **Dr. V. Manikanda Sethupathy**, Assistant Professor, Department of History, Manonmaniam Sundaranar University – Tirunelveli-627 012, TamilNadu., India.
16. **Dr. V. Santhiya**, Assistant Professor, P.G. Department of History, Pasumpon Muthu Ramalinga Thevar College, Melaneelithanallur.
17. **R. Navis Abisha**, Full Time Ph.D Research Scholar, Department of History, Sarah Tucker College, Manonmaniyam Sundaranar University, Tirunelveli.

Index